Fish of Ireland

First published in 1992 by
Appletree Press Ltd
The Old Potato Station
14 Howard Street South
Belfast
BT7 1AP
Tel: +44 (0) 28 90 24 30 74
Fax: +44 (0) 28 90 24 67 56
E-mail: reception@appletree.ie
Web Site: www.appletree.ie

A catalogue record for this book is available from the British Library.

Fish of Ireland

ISBN: 0 86281 958 X

Desk & Marketing Editor: Jean Brown
Editor: Jim Black
Designer: Stuart Wilkinson
Production Manager: Paul McAvoy

9 8 7 6 5 4 3 2 1

AP3244

Fish of Ireland

Ian Hill

I went out to the hazel wood,
Because a fire was in my head,
And cut and peeled a hazel wand
And hooked a berry to a thread;
And when white moths were on the wing,
And moth-like stars were flickering out,
I dropped the berry in a stream
And caught a little silver trout.

W.B. Yeats, *The Song of Wandering Aengus*, from *The Wind Among the Reeds* (1899)

Contents

Contents

Contents

Introduction

The Gulf Stream warms the waters of Ireland's southern and western coasts; the Atlantic pounds the western cliffs, the rocky shores and the long crescents of sandy beaches during the short winter. North and west lie the cold seas. Thus the fish around Ireland's 3,000-mile coastline are a rich and varied mix of warm- and cold-water species. Look at a map of this island country. Round the coast, everywhere is a maze of rivers – many tiny and rushing, some broad and brown, all making their way from the great lakes to the sea. Amongst them, despite – even in green Ireland – the increasing threat of industrial and rural pollution and offshore nets, are some of the best salmon and trout rivers in western Europe. In the centre of the country the Shannon stretches north from Limerick and on to where the lakelands of Cavan and Leitrim merge with the Fermanagh Lakeland, brushing the edges of the Foyle catchment, the River Bann, Lough Neagh, another Bann and the sea again. Pike, resting here amongst the bulrush, the reed mace and the flag iris, feed in the richest coarse fish waters imaginable. Many of these fish are eaten right across Europe, but rarely in Ireland.

Indeed, there appears to be no great tradition in Ireland for eating fish at all. Cecil Woodham Smith wondered why in the classic analysis of the famine years, *The Great Hunger*, and wrote of poor fishing equipment and an inadequate transport system to distribute what fish were caught. The intriguing, if colonialist, *First Report of the Commissioners of Inquiry into the State of the Irish Fisheries*, presented to both Houses of Parliament by Command of His Majesty, puzzled on similar matters and reach much the same conclusions, recommending investment in harbours, fishing gear, boats and training. There was much discussion on preserving stocks and the need for, regrettably, tough action on behalf of the fishery patrols. Change the arcane language, the technical detail, and the same arguments prevail today.

This book sets out to list, illustrate and describe the varieties of fish – over 150 edible species – which live in Irish waters, many of which will provide excellent sport for the angler. The text gives brief details on habitats and seasons, on methods of catching, and, perhaps most important of all, on best methods of cooking. Any angler in Ireland can tell you tales of coming back to port, or of netting or landing his catch, only to be asked by the curious just what kind of fish these are. No one who has travelled in continental Europe and wandered through the fish market in any port, or in any sizeable inland town, can be satisfied by the general standards seen on Irish fishmongers' marble counters. You can eat from a better selection of Irish fish in Madrid.

The book's inspiration comes from the first fish caught on homemade wet-fly in the sea off Ardglass, on worm and spinners in Lough Erne, and from the first salmon on the Bush; as anglers say, tight lines since. It also comes, like all fish books since, from Francis Day's two great volumes, *The Fishes of Great Britain and Ireland*, 1880-84 (the illustrations are also credited to this book), and from two other standard works, both of which acknowledge Day extensively: Alwyne Wheeler's *The Fishes of the British Isles and North-West Europe* and Alan Davidson's *North Atlantic Seafood*. A wider bibliography is given at the end of this guide. The order in which the fifty or so families of fish are presented, and from which the 150-plus species are named, follows current scientific practice.

There is much too much mystique concerning fish cookery; simple is best. If you don't catch the fish, buy only that which has clear convex eyes, pink fresh-smelling gills, bright, tight scales and firm flesh. Scale by scraping forward from the tail. Slit from vent to head, then clean. Small fish can be boned by pressing the split, cleaned fish, back upwards, hard on a board, loosening the backbone and pulling away. Filleting just needs a sharp knife and a little practice cutting away from the backbone. But luckily, many fish taste best cooked on the bone. Cooking times could not be easier: follow the Department of Fisheries of Canada's instructions – **whatever the fish, whatever the method, cook for 10 minutes for each inch (2.5 cm) of thickness measured at its thickest. For baking set at 450°F (230°C).** Allow 8 oz (225 g) of fish flesh per person.

The recipes provided here are only suggestions. Try the recipe for one fish on another within the same family of fish. Fish which might be described as oily can have their flavours enhanced by grilling or baking. Others, with little dark muscle, will dry out if treated the same way. Poaching can enhance delicate flavours. Just remember that fish, when taken directly from the water, cannot be considered safe to eat raw unless frozen for at least five days at -4°F (-20°C), despite the growing fashion for *sashimi*, and despite what old men in distant harbours will tell you about foreign fish-buyers' methods of testing a catch's quality.

Recognition

Note the general form, the presence or absence of gills, the number and position of fins, the number of spines and soft rays in fins, the nature of the scales, and, in certain fish, the teeth. Fin-ray counts, which are used very sparingly in this book, are written in the formula D = dorsal, A = anal. Spiny fin rays are given Roman numerals, soft fin rays Arabic. The illustration opposite gives a 'Naming of Parts'. Fish names throughout the book are given in English, Irish and, for fish-eating travellers, a number of languages abbreviated as follows: *Am.* = American; *Da.* = Danish; *Du.* = Dutch; *Fr.* = French; *Ge.* = German; *It.* = Italian; *No.* = Norwegian; *Po.* = Portuguese; *Sp.* = Spanish; *Sw.* = Swedish; *We.* = Welsh. Scientific names are also included.

Fish are listed by family. The first word of the scientific name indicates the genus, the second word indicates the species within the genus. When an asterisk is inserted, the fish name given in translation is that of the closest relative species of that fish available in the country in question.

Ian Hill
Coney Island, Ardglass & Belfast

Naming of Parts

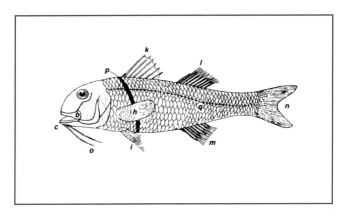

Red Mullet

b, maxilla; *c*, mandible; *o*, barbel; *h*, pectoral fin; *i*, pelvic/ventral fin; *k*, first dorsal fin; *l*, second dorsal fin; *m*, anal fin; *n*, caudal/tail fin; *q*, lateral-line; *p*, lateral-transverse line

Lamprey

Lampern *Loimpre abhann, Péist an dá shúil déag Lampetra fluvialis*
Family: *Petromyzonidae*

Da. Flodlampret; *Du.* Riviereprick; *Fr.* Lamproie Fluviale; *Ge.* Flussneunauge; *It.* Lampreda di Fiume; *No.* Elveniøye; *Po.* Lampreia do Rio; *Sp.* Lamprea de Río; *Sw.* Nahkiinen

Lamprey *Loimpre inhara, Breac an dá shúil déag Petromyzon marinus*

Am. Lamprey; *Da.* Havlampret; *Du.* Zeeprick; *Fr.* Lamproie Marine; *Ge.* Meereunauge; *It.* Lampreda Marina; *No.* Havniøye; *Po.* Lampreia do Mar; *Sp.* Lamprea de Mar; *Sw.* Havsnejonöga

The most primitive of fish, neither the greyish river lamprey, nor the lampern, nor the grey-green brown-spotted sea lamprey are the loveliest of creatures. Lampreys used to be taken right round the Irish coasts and, being anadromous (that is, they run up rivers to spawn), in many of the major rivers, particularly the Bann and the Shannon. The sea lamprey, which has separated dorsal fins, can reach a length of up to 35 in. (90 cm). It is disturbingly slimy and feeds by attaching itself, with a sucker, to other fish – particularly those of the salmon family. It is found on both sides of the Atlantic and its presence in the Great Lakes in North America has done great damage to salmon stocks there. The freshwater, or river lamprey, with a gap between the dorsals, is half the length and less green in colour, as is the even smaller, commoner brook lamprey, *Lampetra planeri, Loimpre shrutháin* in Irish, with its continuous dorsals.

Catch Lamprey are still taken with salmon in nets and in eel weirs, and therefore occasionally appear on a fishmonger's slab or in enterprising restaurants. Surprised anglers may take them on dead baits.

Cook Henry I of England, as every English schoolboy used to know, died of a surfeit of lampreys. However, should you see one of these curiosities, be brave, buy it, skin it, fillet it, cover it in salt for half an hour, then roll the fillets in flour and porridge oats and fry in butter.

Lampern

Lamprey

Dogfish

Lesser-Spotted Dogfish *Freangach, Fiogach beag* *Scyliorhinus canniculus*
Family: *Scliorhinidae*

Da. Smaplettet Rødhaj; *Du*. Hondshaai; *Fr*. Petite Rousette; *Ge*. Kleingefleckter Kaltzenhai; *It*. Gattuchio; *No*. Raudhå; *Po*. Pataroxa; *Sp*. Gato; *Sw*. Småflackig Rödhaj; *We*. Morgi Meiaf

Known variously as the common dogfish, the sandy dog and the rough hound, this gregarious sandy-coloured fish, with lots of brown spots on its back and running up to a maximum length of about 30 in. (75 cm) is obviously a little member of the shark family. It is ubiquitous in Irish and indeed in most European coastal waters. The greater-spotted dogfish, nurse hound, bull huss or huss, *Scyliorhinus stellaris* – *madra mór* in Irish – greater in both overall size and in the size of its spots, is much less common. Unlike the smaller species, its nasal flaps are separate and not continuous. The black-mouthed dogfish, *Galeus melastomus* – *fidéog* in Irish – has much bolder patterning, and inside its mouth is black. As a child you will have picked up its shiny brown egg cases (mermaids' purses) on the beach after a storm.

Catch The problem for most boat-anglers is not how to catch a dogfish but how not to catch them in dozens. Anglers, bottom-fishing for flatfish over sandy banks, can run into packs of what they dismissively refer to as doggies, which take every bait. The larger bull huss is more likely to be caught over rough or rocky ground. All dogfish are normally unfussy and nocturnal feeders, feeding on crabs, whelks, worms, sand-eels and gobies, and quite often can be observed on a calm day, apparently sleeping on the bottom. If catching one for the first time, make sure to secure its tail before removing the hook – or it will wrap its tail around your wrist and scar painfully with its sandpaper skin. In seaboard communities the skins were used as fine sandpaper.

Cook We have all been eating doggies for years in these islands, though few of us may know it. The rock salmon, or rock eel, of the traditional fish and chips shops, has always been, in reality, the doggie. Skin by making an incision right round behind the head and pull off the skin using a cloth for grip and protection. Dip in beaten egg and breadcrumbs, deep-fry or bake.

Lesser-Spotted Dogfish

Greater-Spotted Dogfish

Black-Mouthed Dogfish

Mackerel & other Sharks

Porbeagle *Craosaire sgadán* *Lamna nasus* Family: *Isuridae*

Am. Mackerel Shark; *Da.* Sildehaj; *Du.* Neushaai; *Fr.* Taupe; *Ge.* Heringshai; *It.* Smeriglio; *No.* Håbrann; *Po.* Anequim; *Sp.* Marrajo; *Sw.* Sillhaj; *We.* Morgi Mawr

This stout blue-grey shark with surprisingly large eyes is found on both sides of the Atlantic. It can grow up to 400 lb (180 kg), and if you ever get close enough to one when it is dead, you will be able to make out the small extra cusps at the base of its teeth, a feature which helps distinguish it from other large sharks. The first dorsal is directly above the pectoral fin. The porbeagle's name in English may have come from compounding porpoise and beagle, a hunting dog. Its name in French, *taupe*, no doubt comes from its fashionable colour. In the illustration, the first dorsal fin is uncharacteristically far back.

Mako *Isurus oxyrincus* Family: *Isuridae*

Fr. Lamie; *No.* Makrellhai

The mako, which is quite similar but slightly slimmer, with smaller eyes and the first dorsal fin rising behind the start of the pectoral fin, is more blue in colour, though it is not the distantly related blue shark (*see page 23*).

Six-Gilled Shark *Craosaire sé geolbhach* *Hexancus griseus*
Family: *Notianoidae*

Da. Seksgaellet Haj; *Fr.* Griset; *Ge.* Grauhai; *It.* Squalo Cappotiatto; *No.* Kamtannet Gråhai; *Sp.* Cañabota

One of the most primitive of these primitive of these primitive fish, the six-gilled shark has six obvious gills and a single dorsal fin.

Hammerhead Shark *Craosaire ceann casúir* *Sphyrna zygaena*
Family: *Sphyrnidae*

Da. Hammerhaj; *Du.* Hamerhaai; *Fr.* Marteau; *Ge.* Hammerhai; *It.* Pesce Martello; *Po.* Cornuda; *Sp.* Pez Martillo

The hammerhead shark has not yet been caught off the coasts of Ireland, but it surely will one day.

Basking Shark *Liamhán gréine* *Cetorhinus maximus* Family: *Cetorhinidae*

Da. Brugde; *Du.* Reuzenhaai; *Fr.* Requin; *Ge.* Riesenhai; *It.* Squalo Elephante; *No.* Brugde; *Sp.* Peregrino

Feeding on plankton, the basking shark was, until recently, hunted commercially off Achill Island for its unique oil.

Catch There has been an expansion in the provision of well-equipped charter-boat fishing off the west and south-west coasts of Ireland, and a number of boats specialise in summer shark-fishing. After putting out rubby-dubby, trolling with IGFA 30 lb (14 kg) tackle, ending with 400 lb (180 kg) nylon and hooks on a wire trace baited with whole fish, you can be productive with the right skipper at the wheel. The Irish record fish, 365 lb (165 kg), was taken off Achill Island in 1932.

Cook Once despised, particularly in Ireland, shark steaks are now beginning to make their way on to the menus of fashionable, yet inexpensive, bistros and into the freezers of enterprising fishmongers. Though it would be an unusual sport-fisher who would carve himself one from his catch on the spot, there is not doubt that shark steaks, hot-smoked or grilled, then sprinkled with lemon juice, are excellent fare.

Porbeagle

Mackerel & other Sharks

Six-Gilled Shark

Hammerhead Shark

Basking Shark

Tope & Blue Shark

Tope *Gearrthóir, Madra gorm, Fámaire Gaelorhinus galus*
Family: *Carcharinidae*

Da. Graahaj; *Du.* Ruwehaai; *Fr.* Milandre; *Ge.* Hundhai; *It.* Canesca; *No.* Graahai; *Sp.* Cazón

Ironically known as Sweet William for its ammoniacal aroma, this vigorous shark is of an elegant pale-grey colour and runs up to 75 lb (34 kg). Its range covers the east but not west Atlantic, plus the Mediterranean. A distinguishing feature is the definite notch in the tail fin.

Smooth Hound / Sweet William *Scoirneach, Madar glas Mustelus asterias*
Family: *Triakidae*

Da. Glathaj; *D.* Toonhaai; *Fr.* Emmisole; *Ge.* Glatthai; *It.* Palombo; *Po.* Cação; *Sp.* Musola

The smooth hound looks like a tope with white spots.

Blue Shark *Siorc gorm, Craosaire gorm Prionace glauca*
Family: *Carcharinidae*

Da. Blaahaj; *Du.* Blauwe Haai; *Fr.* Requin Bleu; *Ge.* Blauer Hai; *It.* Verdesca; *No.* Blaahai; *Sp.* Tintorera

The blue, which often gets caught in fishing nets, is the shark with long, slender pectoral fins.

Thresher Shark *Craosaire sionnach Alopias vulpinus* Family: *Alopiidae*

Da. Raevehai; *Du.* Voshaai; *Fr.* Reynard de Mar; *Ge.* Fuchshai; *It.* Squalo Volpe; *No.* Raevehai; *Sp.* Pez Zorro

The thresher is, by contrast, distinguished by its dramatic tail. It grows to over 1,000 lb (453 kg).

Catch Tope run up the big Irish estuaries to breed in summer, and the later we go around the coast, clockwise from the south west, the later is the run. Catching the big ones is a specialist activity. The best bait is a whole mackerel, backbone removed, one 4/0 hook through its head, another secure in one of the fillets – both of which are flapping in the tide. A sinker of 4 to 6 oz (113-170 g)

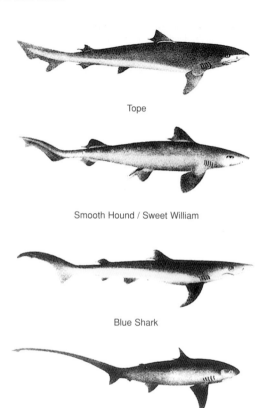

Tope

Smooth Hound / Sweet William

Blue Shark

Thresher Shark

will suffice. Keep your nerve, let the fish make its 100-200 metre run with the bait, time your strike accurately for the second run and you have a great fight on your hands, using 20 lb (9 kg) tackle with a 50lb (22.5 kg) wire trace attached to a few terminal metres of 60 lb (27 kg) nylon. All fish must be released for conservation reasons. Wet canvas slings are provided for the weigh-in on the best-equipped boats, though to beat the Irish record of 66.8 lb (30.191 kg), you have to get your fish shore-weighed and released live again. Don't try if you have any doubts.

Cook Please don't, unless it is smooth hound. Then treat as doggie.

Spiny Shark

Spur Dog *Fíogach gobach Squalus acanthais* Family: *Squaloidae*

Am. Spiny Dogfish; *Da.* Pighaj; *Du.* Doornhai; *Fr.* Aiguillat; *Ge.* Gemeiner Dornhai; *It.* Spinarolo; *No.* Pigghà; *Po.* Galhudo; *Sp.* Agulat, Mielga; *Sw.* Pigghaj; *We.* Ci Piog

The spur dog, which takes its name from the big, strong, triangular-and-grooved spines almost hidden in its two dorsal fins, is probably the most common of the small spiny sharks on both sides of the Atlantic and in the Mediterranean. It grows slowly, taking up to twenty-five years to reach its maximum length of around 47 in. (120 cm). It is grey to black topside, almost white underneath. The young are expelled from the female's body live, and not as eggs. Its skin also was once used as sandpaper, the liver for lamp oil in rural seaboard communities.

Bramble / Spiny Shark *Craosaire dris Echinorhinus brucus*

Fr. Bouclé; *Ge.* Stachelhai; *It.* Ronco; *Sp.* Pez Tachuela

With two curious far-back dorsal fins and skin covered in spiny bucklers, the bramble is easily recognised.

Greenland Shark *Craosaire Ghraonlainn Somniosus microcephalus*

Da. Havkel; *Du.* Apekalle; *Fr.* Leiche; *Ge.* Eishai; *It.* Squalo di Groenlandia; *No.* Haakjaerring; *Sp.* Tiburón Boreal

A rare visitor, the big clumsy-looking Greenland has no anal fin and has been caught in Scottish waters; it should be available off Rathlin and Fanad.

Other spiny sharks are the velvet belly, *Etmopterus spinax*, and the politically incorrectly named *Darkie Charlie*, with its dark-brown skin and white lips (*Dalatias licha*).

Catch Distributed widely around Irish coasts, spur dogs are caught mostly on hooks baited with mackerel strip, and keen anglers set themselves targets of a 12 lb (5.43 kg) fish. The Irish record is an 18 lb 12 oz (8.45 kg) fish caught off Bantry in 1977. The despicable and barbaric practice of wrenching or cutting off the fish's spines (which are potentially dangerous to the angler, as the fish, like other sharks, winds its body round the captor's wrist) and returning it live to the sea as an act of macho barbarity is the type of activity which gives angling a bad name.

Cook Once sold dried and salted, spur-dog flesh has a robust flavour, firm texture, moderate fat content and an off-white colour when cooked. It is often sautéed or deep-fried. Before cooking, the steaks or fillets should be left in salt for an hour. It can also be casseroled successfully at very low heat with cooking oil, lots of black pepper, a little onion (for moisture) and plenty of parsley.

Spur Dog

Bramble / Siny Shark

Greenland Shark

Monkfish

Monkfish *Bráithair* *Squatina squatina*
Family: *Squatinidae*

Am. Angel Shark*; *Da.* Havengle; *Du.* Zeeëngle; *Fr.* Ange de Mer; *Ge.* Meerengel; *It.* Squadro; *Po.* Peixe Anjo; *Sp.* Angelote; *We.* Maelgi

Called monkfish in English and Irish from the presence of cowl-like shapes around its head, and angel shark because of its wings, this strange and baroque-looking brown-mottled fish is indeed a member of the shark family, though it appears a cross between a shark and a skate. It is, as its shape suggests, a bottom-feeder, dining voraciously on small flatfish and shellfish. Not surprisingly, it is very tasty. The monkfish can grow to a length of about 6.5 ft (2 m) and weigh up to 100 lb (45.4 kg). It should not be confused (though fishmongers and restaurants still do so) with the anglerfish (*see page 124*). The skin was once used to cover sword handles. Confined to the eastern Atlantic and Mediterranean, it has a close relation in *Squatina dumerili** in the western Atlantic.

Catch Casual reading of statistics suggests that monkfish have been caught commercially around Irish shores in large numbers since unscrupulous restaurateurs took to substituting the monk's firm flesh for that of more expensive lobster. **However, it is really the anglerfish which is landed in quantity and marketed as monkfish.** Though dull and heavy, sport-anglers would like to catch more, both for its taste and its bizarre appearance. The usual bait is mackerel, and the Irish record stands at 73 lb (33 kg). Fenit is the favoured port.

Cook Monkfish may certainly be fried or sautéed, but benefits most from gentle poaching. Cut into larger than bite-sized slices, simmer in a good fish stock with cloves, peppercorns, salt and vinegar. Serve with a robustly tasting, colourful sauce, preferably tomato- or fruit-based (gooseberry, redcurrant). It can also be baked in a buttered dish, after seasoning, being well soaked in lemon juice. Later it can be topped with a simple egg-and-flour mix and popped back in for 10 minutes.

Skate

Common Skate *Scalaphort, Sciata Raja batis*
Family: *Rajidae*

Am. Barndoor Skate*, *Da.* Skade; *Du.* Vleet; *Fr.* Pocheteau; *Ge.* Glattroche; *It.* Razza Bavosa; *No.* Glattskate; *Po.* Raia; *Sp.* Noriega; *Sw.* Slatrokka

The terms skate and ray, of related though different families, are often interchanged, and in America the term ray is usually used for all members of the families of these cartilaginous fish. The big, the California, the clearnose, the cownose, the little, the thorny and the winter are American skate species; the common, the longnose and the white are found only on the east side of the Atlantic. The leading edge of the skate wing is entirely concave; that of the ray is convex, nearest the snout. In addition, the word ray is generally used to indicate smaller species. The common skate weighs up to 200 lb (90 kg), is grey above and is white bellied with black-marked pores.

White Skate *Scalaphort bán Raja alba*

Fr. Raie Bordée; *It.* Razza Bianca; *Sp.* Raya Blanca

This big grey-white skate has a white underside with a black border, but no black on the pores.

Long-Nosed Skate *Scalaphort fadsrón Raja oxyrinchus*

Du. Scherpsnuit; *Fr.* Raie Capucin; *Ge.* Spitzschnauziger Roche; *It.* Razza Monaca; *No.* Plogskate; *Sp.* Picón

The long-nosed skate is a deep-water species, grey brown with pale spots which fade on capture.

Shagreen Ray *Roc grainneach Raja fullonica*

Da. Gjogerokken; *Du.* Kaardrog; *Fr.* Raie Chardon; *Ge.* Chagrinroche; *It.* Razza Spinosa; *No.* Naebskate; *Sp.* Raya Caradore

Looking more like a small skate than a ray, this fish has a rough upperside and a white underside with no dark pores. It grows to 3 ft (1 m).

Catch Deep-water fish, big skate can be caught with great patience off Cork and Galway and in deep holes in sea loughs, such as Strangford, using whole mackerel or whiting on a metal trace at slack water on the near tide. These huge fish sweep the bait towards their mouths, and so, after an initial tug, anglers may well think they are caught on a rock, pinned down by the huge weight and suction of the fish spread on the sand. The trick is to drop a weight down the line, bumping the fish on its nose, surprising it enough to leave the bottom briefly. After that, it is a long, slow pump to the surface. Average skate of 80 lb (36 kg) can be taken on 30 lb (14 kg) tackle. Pier fishing at Fenit works too.

Cook The common skate should be a protected species in all Irish waters, but 'skate' wings, from many related species, are common in fishmongers. Cook in a black butter sauce, as for thornback ray (*see page 32*), or cut into 4-cm pieces. Simmer in a court-bouillon with mace and nutmeg 15 minutes, reduce, add a knob of butter and stir in half a pint of cream.

Common Skate

Long-Nosed Skate

Ray

Thornback Ray / Roker *Roc garbh Raja clavata* Family: *Rajidae*

Am. Thorny Ray*; *Da*. Sømrokke; *Du*. Stekelrog; *Fr*. Raie Bouclée; *Ge*. Keulenrochen; *It*. Razza Chiodata; *No*. Piggskate; *Po*. Raia Pregada; *Sp*. Raya de Clavos; *Sw*. Knaggrocka; *We*. Cath Fôr

Grey or fawn, mottled brown, growing up to 33 in. (83 cm), this ray is easily distinguished by its 'thorns' or spines. These are most prominent and dangerous along the tail, but are also found on the snout, around the eyes and down the back. Note the similarity between the Irish *roc* and the English roker – the Irish name means rough ray. It is quite common in Irish waters and its range runs from Norway to the Mediterranean. Like all sharks, rays and skates, the thornback can have an ammoniacal smell. This is natural and due to the way these fish use urea to maintain their osmotic balance. All sea fish have less salt in their bodies than in the sea and they tend to lose water, by what is called osmosis, to the sea. To maintain a healthy balance, bony fish use chloride cells in their gills, while fish with cartilage instead of bones use urea. These fish taste best when dead for two days when the urea has been discharged.

Catch The thornback ray is caught from boats, on shallow, sandy bottoms, often at the turn of the tide where two currents meet, in summer. It is especially partial to soft shell crab, ragworm and shellfish bait. Many anglers believe it necessary to bleed the fish immediately after catching to improve the taste. Courtmacsherry, Greystones and Portrush are good bases to hunt the tasty thornback. A number of other rays, such as the undulate (Ir. *roc dubhstríocha*, i.e. dark-streaked ray), as well as those following are caught here in like fashion.

Cuckoo Ray *Roc na súl dubh* *Raja naevus*

Du. Koekoeksrog; *Fr*. Raie Fleurie; *Ge*. Kuckucksroche; *It*. Razza Fiorita; *Sp*. Raya Santiaguesa

The cuckoo ray is yellow brown with a black-and-yellow squiggly spot on the wings.

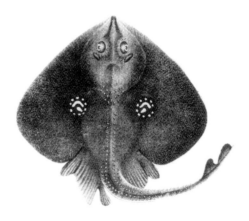

Homelyn / Spotted Ray *Roc breac, Roc mín Raja monyagui*

Du. Gladde Rog; *Fr*. Raie Douce; *Ge*. Geflechter Roche; *It*. Razza Maculata; *Po*. Raia Pintada; *Sp*. Raya Pintada

The homelyn is similar to the blonde ray, although the spots do not reach the trailing edge.

Painted Ray *Roc bán-stríocta Raja microocellata*

Du. Uilrog; *Fr*. Raie Mêlée

Grey with white spots and lines.

Blonde Ray *Roc fionn Raja brachyura* Family: *Rajidae*

Du. Blonde Rog; *Fr*. Raie Blanche; *Ge*. Blonde; *It*. Razza a Coda Corta; *Sp*. Raya Boca de Rosa

The blond ray grows to 40 lb (18 kg) and is fawn with small dark spots running to trailing edge.

Starry Ray *Raja radiata*

Da. Taerbe; *Du*. Keilrog; *Fr*. Raie Radiée; *Ge*. Sternroche; *No*. Kloskate; *Sw*. Klorocka

Also found off the American north Atlantic shores, its upper surface is dotted with curved spines on ribbed bases. The starry ray grows to 2 ft (60 cm).

Electric Ray *Craimpiasc Torpedo nobiliana* Family: *Torpedinidae*

Da. Elektrisk Rokke; *Du*. Electrieke Rog; *Fr*. Torpille; *Ge*. Zitteroche; *It*. Torpedino; *Sp*. Tremiegla

Grey brown, smooth and circular, the electric ray has two dorsals on its tail and grows to 100 lb (45 kg).

Homelyn / Spotted Ray

Starry Ray

Eagle Ray *Roc iolar* *Myliobatis aquila* Family: *Myliobatoidae*

Da. Ørnerokke; *Du*. Groote Pijlstaart; *Fr*. Aigle de Mer; *Ge*. Alderroche; *It*. Aquila di Mare; *No*. Örneskate; *Sp*. Aquila de Mar

With its pointed wings and prominent elevated head, the eagle ray grows to 5 ft (1.5 m).

Devil Ray *Deilgín deamhain* *Mobula mobular* Family: *Myliobatoidae*

Du. Duivelsrog; *Fr*. Mante; *Ge*. Teufelsroche; *It*. Manta; *Sp*. Manta

With a whip-like spurred tail and 'horned' head, this is a true manta.

Sting Ray *Roc an ghaith nimhe* *Dasyatis pastinaca* Family: *Myliobatoidae*

Da. Pilrokke; *Du*. Pijlstaart; *Fr*. Pastenauge; *Ge*. Gemeiner Stechroche; *It*. Pastinacha; *Sp*. Pastinaca

At 70 lb (32 kg), the sting ray's venomous spined tail is really dangerous.

Cook The wings of various rays and skates, variously and casually named, are widely available in fishmongers, but the cheeks (a real delight) and delicious knobs from the tail of the thornback come only courtesy of your favourite angler. You need about 8 oz (227 g) of fish per person, and the flesh should be a slight pink. Place the wings in a large pan with a chopped onion, 2 tbsp of wine vinegar, lemon juice, a bay leaf and a scattering of peppercorns. Cover with water. Simmer gently. Melt 4 oz (113 g) of butter in another pan until it turns the colour of hazelnuts, add a handful of chopped parsley, a splash of vinegar, a dozen or so capers; pour over the cooked fish when transferred to a serving dish.

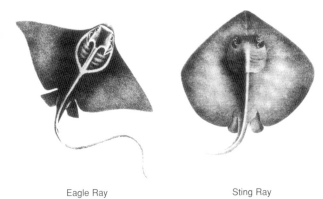

Eagle Ray   Sting Ray

Devil Ray

Shad

Twaite Shad *Sead fhallacsach, Capall cnámhach Allosa fallax fallax*
Family: *Culpeidae*

A beautiful herring-like fish with big scales, startlingly blue black and shiny on the back, the belly silver, the twaite is easily distinguished from the related allis shad, *Alosa alosa*, by the line of spots along its side. The twaite reaches a length of 20 in. (50 cm), the allis 24 in. (60 cm). The allis is caught only in estuaries in the south west of Ireland, when it comes up to spawn in May; the twaite ranges further north. Ireland has its own shad, the Killarney, or *gobhar*, 9 in. (23 cm), a landlocked sub-species – *Alosa fallax killarnensis*. The Irish name for the twaite shad means 'bony horse', though Day gives it as 'bony Norseman'.

Catch Traditionally shad were caught in funnel-shaped basket-work traps, faced upstream to catch the fish on the ebb tide. German commercial fishermen attached bells to their nets in the belief that shad liked quiet musical sounds. Anglers take them on small spinners, worked fast, or fly-fishing using streamer flies or nymphs. Sea slaters, float-fished on 3 lb (1.3 kg) line, have worked in the Barrow, Suir and Slaney.

Cook The delicious shad is a most bony fish. However, as the bones dissolve, or at least soften to the state of those in tinned pilchards, after prolonged contact with sorrel, the answer is to place the fish on a bed of sorrel, wrap it in foil with butter, salt and pepper and cook, very slowly, for up to 4 hours. By the skilled, the back and connected fin bones can be removed before cooking. Steam a leek, an onion and a carrot over a court-bouillon in a fish kettle. Add the fillets, dredged in coarse salt, after 15 minutes. After 5 minutes, remove the fish, blend the vegetables with a cup of the court-bouillon, and reheat with 3 oz (85 g) of butter to make a fine sauce. Alternatively, just fry the roes in butter.

Herring

Herring *Scadán Clupea harengus*
Family: *Clupeidae*

Am. Atlantic Herring; *Da*. Sild; *Du*. Haring; *Fr*. Hareng; *Ge*. Hering; *It*. Aringa; *Sp*. Arengue; *Sw*. Sill; *We*. Pennog

The roe of a herring is diuretic. The whole herring well salted, and applied to the soles of the feet draws humours from the head, mitigates feverish heats, and cures a megrim. The brine or pickle is used in clysters for the sciatica and dropsy, mixt with honey, it cleanses ulcers, dispels strumas, and is good against the Quinsy.

Thus wrote John K'eogh, Chaplain to the Rt Hon. Baron of Kingston in his *Zoologiina Medicalis Hibernica, 1793.*

Catch There is sport to be had of a summer's evening when the herring come close to shore. The sea sits flat and calm, and as the coast disappears in the early haze, the only sound is the *phutt* of the boat's engine. Eyes scan the seas for diving terns, bright, vigorous pointers to the shoals. Feathers, jigged, bring forth the silver darlings, wriggling, slapping, to the boat's side. Content yourself with what you will eat fresh that evening, or in the morning. The Irish record line-caught fish stands at 15 oz (425 g), taken off Rathlin Island, its length 15 in. (38 cm).

Cook Gutted, tossed in the hottest of pans which has been moistened with bacon fat, cooked until the outside is crisp and brown as toast, served with new potatoes, boiled in their jackets, split with just a knob of butter each, a sprig of parsley, a wedge of lemon, a pinch of salt – could paradise be half as nice? An indulgence would be to roll the brace of herring in seasoned oatmeal. Hedonists brush the fish with mustard first. The potatoes should be Pentlands, great balls of flour. Sauté roes in butter. Mill black pepper over them, serve on toast.

Pilchard (adult) / Sardine (young) *Pilséar / Sairdín Clupea pilchardus*
Family: *Clupidae*

Am. False Pilchard*; *Da.* Sardin; *Du.* Pelser, Sardien; *Fr.* Sardine; *Ge.* Sardine; *No.* Sardin; *It.* Sardina; *Po.* Sardina; *Sp.* Sardina; *We.* Pennog Mair

A shy fish, the sardine, or pilchard, can be scared off by gunfire. In 1689 the then archbishop of Dublin related how the sea battle in Bantry Bay between the French and English scared fish off for the whole season. Gentlemen firing their guns from yachts in Dublin Bay (for whatever reason) had similar effects. So, when does this delicious green-backed, yellow-sided, silver-bellied, large-scaled member of the herring family stop being a sardine and grow up to be a pilchard? Hard to tell, and anyway Americans tin any small member of the herring family except their own flavourless related species as sardines. Suffice it to say sardines are sardine-tin size; pilchards can grow up to 11 in. (28 cm).

Catch Though grossly over-fished, anglers may catch pilchard on herring strip.

Cook This delightful fish is more likely to be taken at table on an Iberian holiday or bought, frozen, from a good fishmonger. The essential qualities suffer little from freezing. Brush with olive oil; grill, preferably over charcoal. Eat with your fingers, then, if the company prompts it, kiss your dinner companion's sticky lips.

Sprat *Salán, Sprot Sprattus sprattus*

Da. Brisling; *Du.* Sprotte; *Fr.* Sprat; *Ge.* Sprotte; *It.* Spratto; *No.* Brisling; *Po.* Espadilha; *Sp.* Espadín; *Sw.* Skarpsill; *We.* Coog Pennog

The much smaller sprat has a shorter, deeper body and is distinguished by having its pelvic fin just in advance of its dorsal. When fresh it is grilled or sautéed, but traditionally it is found in tins marked Brisling, smoked.

Anchovy *Ainseabhaí Engraulis encrasicolus*

Am. Striped Anchovy*; *Da*. Ansjos; *Du*. Ansjovis; *Fr*. Anchois; *Ge*. Sardelle; *Po*. Biqueirâo; *Sp*. Boquerón; *We*. Brwyniad

A rare visitor to Irish shores, this little greeny-blue fish, with the silver belly and the distinctively shaped heavy snout, is caught occasionally by sport-fishers as is, in American waters, its American cousin* *Anchoa hepsetus*. Hot-smoked, grilled or dried, it never loses its distinctive flavour, even in the tinned form, which you toss into *salade niçoise* or on to your omelettes. The anchovy is at its best filleted, fried in oil, then marinated in a mix of onion, garlic, carrot, salt, bay leaf, thyme, chilli, wine vinegar, lemon juice and water, which has been boiled, cooled, poured over the fish, then refrigerated for two weeks.

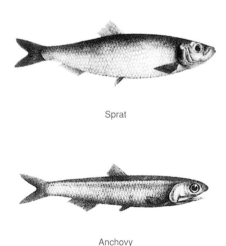

Sprat

Anchovy

41

Whitefish

Pollan *Pollán Coregonus autumnalis pollan*
Family: *Coregonidae*

Am. Whitefish*; *Fr.* Bondell**, Petite Mârene**; *Ge.* Kleine Marane**; *Sw.* Sikolja**

Whitefish have silvery bodies and an adipose fin typical of the salmon family. Many are in land-locked lakes. Pollan, the Irish representative, have been taken in Lough Neagh, Lough Erne, Lough Ree and Lough Derg, and a number of smaller lakes. A letter to the lord bishop of Clogher, dated 12 February 1712, describes them as 'much in shape and in bigness like to the largest smelts, full of very large bright scales, and pleasant meat, being eat fresh'. There is a bluish tinge to the back, and the fins darken towards the edges. It is most closely related to those of Siberia and Alaska, having migrated here after the last Ice Age, 10,000 years ago, and colonised Ireland by swimming up the Shannon. They reach about 10 in. (25 cm), weighing 6 oz (170 g). Broad, cisco, humpback, inconnu, lake and mountain whitefish are marketed in America*. The European continental vendace** is another close relative, as are the English freshwater houting, the Scots powan and the Welsh *schelly*, or *gwyniad*.

Catch Pollan are taken on the fly at dusk, or on maggot or tiny blood worm fished deep. In Lough Neagh they feed on tiny freshwater shrimp, *Mystis relicta;* in Lough Derg on *Daphnia longispina*. Commercial nets take them in late summer and autumn dusks, and a small market for them still exists, particularly from the Lough Neagh fishery from where they were regularly transported to Lancashire. They can still be bought, in season, in good Belfast fish shops.

Cook Related to both trout and herring, pollan, around Lough Neagh, are cooked in manners suitable to either, but only when very fresh, as the flesh softens quickly.

Smelt

Smelt / Sparling *Cualarach, Smealt* Osmerus eperlanus
Family: *Osmeridae*

Am. Rainbow Smelt*; *Da.* Smelt; *Du.* Spiering; *Fr.* Éperlan; *Ge.* Stint; *It.* Sperlano; *Sp.* Eperláno; *Sw.* Nors

Distantly related to herring, salmon and whitefish, the smelt – in Ireland found only in the Shannon estuary – is a slim silver fish of around 6 in. (15 cm), with a brilliant silver side stripe and smelling of cucumber, violets or rushes. Hence the name. There is a small adipose fin far behind the dorsal. The American rainbow smelt*, *Osmerus mordax*, is well regarded. These smelt are no relation to the sand-smelt, or atherine.

Catch Smelt are predators feeding on young fish and shrimp, but rarely worms. They tolerate low salinity and come well up the Shannon in shoals from May to August. Best caught at night from a lighted boat to attract their attention, and with a net, they can also be taken on light tackle, float-fishing with tiny hooks.

Cook Day notes that split and dried, smelt are a great delight, downed with the morning dram. Wash and dry the fish, gut through the gills if you wish, roll in seasoned flour, then fry in a mixture of oil and butter. Sprinkle with lemon. Better still, skewer, dip in milk, then flour before deep-frying. Delicious. Argentines, described overleaf, are worth frying, though not so delicious.

Argentine *Airgeadúil* *Argentina silus* Family: *Argentinidae*

Da. Guldlaks; *Du.* Zilvervis; *Fr.* Argentine; *Ge.* Glasauge; *No.* Stavsild; *Po.* Biqueirâo Branco; *Sp.* Pez de Plata; *Sw.* Guidlax

Growing to 20 in. (50 cm), this yellowy fish with its silvery sheen is widely distributed across the northern Atlantic. Feeding on worms and small fish, it may be caught accidentally, bottom-fishing.

Salmon

Salmon *Bradán* *Salmo salar* Family: *Salmonidae*

Da. Lax; *Du.* Zalm; *Fr.* Saumon; *Ge.* Lachs; *It.* Salmone de Reno; *No.* Laks; *Po.* Salmão; *Sp.* Salmón; *Sw.* Lax; *We.* Eog

The female Irish salmon digs a redd in up-river gravel, releasing spawn when her mate joins her to eject his milt. Three months later, the alevins emerge, grow to fry, then to parr. A year or two later the finger-length black-and-red spotted trout-like parr migrate to sea, changing to elegant silvery smolts as they go. A year and 2,000 nautical miles later, they come back again to the same river as grilse, weighing 2 to 10 lb (1 to 4 kg). Or they may not return until later years as adult fish, 3 ft (1 m) long. If they survive the Atlantic nets, the estuarial nets, the poacher and the rich angler, they spawn and mostly perish. A few survive as kelts. A fresh-run salmon is all blue and silver. At spawning the female is dull and leaden coloured, the male red-and-orange mottled with a hooked lower jaw. The Atlantic salmon is also caught in North American waters, and the Pacific has a number of separate species; cherry, chinook, chum, coho, pink and sockeye. Recent genetic research points to two Irish races – the celtic in the north west, the boreal in the south. One humpback salmon, *Oncorhyncus gorbusca*, has been recorded from the Moy.

Catch The great salmon rivers of Galway and Mayo, Donegal, Derry and Antrim are amongst Europe's best. You can fish the Corrib in the middle of Galway City, or at the great weir at Carnroe on the Bann, and catch fish you will never forget, on fly or shrimp, spinner or worm, according to local custom. A spinner whimsically referred to in Ireland as a 'flying condom' is almost too deadly to be sporting. A fresh wind, scattered cloud, water rising after rain and a delayed strike make for more fish taken. River spring-runs start, for some, on 1 January; the last in October for others. There are the great lakes, Corrib and Melvin, amongst many.

Cook A taste of the wild will spoil your enjoyment of much of the farmed. Poach whole fish in a court-bouillon. Serve hot or cold with new potatoes. Grill steaks. Make gravlax (*see page 46*).

Trout

Sea Trout *Breac geal   Salmo trutta trutta*
Family: *Salmonidae*

Da. Havørred; *Du.* Zeeforel; *Fr.* Truite de Mer; *Ge.* Meerforelle; *It.* Trota di Mare; *No.* Sjøaure; *Po.* Truta Marisca; *Sp.* Trucha Marina; *Sw.* Öring; *We.* Sewin

Brown Trout *Breac donn   Salmo trutta fario*

Da. Baekørred; *Du.* Beekforel; *Fr.* Truite; *Ge.* Bachforelle; *It.* Trota; *No.* Ørret; *Po.* Truta; *Sp.* Trucha; *Sw.* Bäcköring

It will surprise many that the bluey-silvery sea trout with its tiny x-shaped black spots is really the same species as the wild brown trout – olive, bronzed, golden with a scattering of dark-and-red spots. Diet, habitat and genetics control the colouring in a species whose range runs from Africa to Iceland and whose variations include big lake trout, river trout and the migratory sea trout. The size can be from 2 oz (57 g) to 20 lb (9 kg). In Lough Melvin alone there are five sub-species, as well as charr and salmon: the sonaghan, *S.t. nigripinnis*, silver with black fins and black-and-red spots; the gillaroo, *S.t. stomachicus*, golden with orange spots; the ferox, *S.t. ferox*, larger mouthed, fewer spots; as well as the brown and sea trout. They maintain their genetic integrity by different spawning habits. Big loughs have huge fish. Sea trout migrate to sea, brown trout do not. Slob trout may be hybrids.

Catch Trout will, in the right conditions, take any bait, but the sport-angler goes mainly for dry- or wet-fly fishing. The artificial dry-fly, on the surface of the water, imitates members of the mayfly or sedge fly families; the wet-fly, moving, imitates insect larvae or small fish. Dapping with mayfly on a wind-blown, billowing line is a particularly Irish delight. Big trout are taken by trolling lures on big lakes. Reared rainbows are caught in 'put-and-take' lakes.

Cook The ubiquitous rainbow (originally Californian, now farmed over Europe) is not, when farmed, the best of fish. The flesh is often dull and flaccid. Wild brownies should be grilled or foil-baked with butter and herbs. Sea trout make magical gravlax. Place one boned fillet, skin down, in a glass casserole. Cover with dill, 4 tbsp sea salt, 1.5 tbsp caster sugar and lots of crushed peppercorns. Cover with the other fillet, skin up. Weigh down, refrigerate for two days, turning four times. Slice as smoked salmon. Serve with mustard sauce: 4 tbsp Dijon mustard, 1 tsp mustard powder, 1 tbsp caster sugar, 2 tbsp white vinegar, 4 tbsp chopped dill (or 1 tbsp of crushed seeds), and 6 tbsp oil, whisked and beaten.

Sea Trout

Brown Trout

Ferox

Sonaghan

Slob Trout

Charr

Charr *Breac dearg, Ruabhreac Salvelinus alpinus* Family: *Salmonidae*

Charr, trout-like fish, usually grow in Ireland to around 2 lb (0.9 kg). Generally they are olive to blue on top, with pale spots in the darkest areas and paler on the sides. Breeding males become red (*dearg* means 'red' in Irish) to orange along the belly. Anglers recognise a number of regional charr variations: Cole's in loughs Conn, Eske, Dan, Corrib and Mask; Gray's in Lough Melvin; dwarf Trevelyan's in Lough Finn; the blue-nosed in Wicklow and Killarney lakes; the dwarf Coomasaharn in Lough Coomasaharn. The jury is still deliberating on whether these are genetically distinct species. Found in cold waters, they range across the Arctic and further south in a maze of related species. Like trout, they spawn in redds, usually at night in March or September.

Catch Traditionally lake charr were taken by trolling – on swivels – several small copper and silver spoons, droppers spaced 3 m (10 ft) apart, and weighted line at about 30 m deep, an oarsman rowing the boat slowly. A tiny bell was attached to a shaped board to keep the line down. In some lakes, charr will take brandlings deep, or rise to the fly on warm evenings, seeking *Daphnia* which they suck at slowly, not snatching like a trout. In Lough Owel they can run to 3 lb (1.4 kg).

Cook The charr's firm, pink flesh can be treated like a trout's; even better, poach gently, then separate the flesh from the bones before blending it slowly, using a fork, with melted butter, a pinch of nutmeg, a dash of mace, a grinding of black pepper. Place in a ramekin, seal with melted butter. Charr, thus potted and topped with a sprig of parsley, a wedge of lemon and served with buttered wheaten toast, is a delight.

Pike

Pike *Liús Essox lucius* Family: *Escocidae*

This mottled-olive carnivorous torpedo, with the fierce teeth and duck-billed snout, rests on the bottom of most Irish fresh waters waiting to pounce on passing prey. It is, however, scarce in Donegal, Cork, Kerry and Wicklow. Small fish, a frog, a young moorhen, even – old men in pubs will tell you – a passing dog are considered its prey. The river record is 42 lb (19 kg), the lake 41 lb (18.61 kg). Legends speak of 100 lb (45 kg) fish. Knox, in his history of Co. Down, cites 350 lb (158 kg). Nevertheless, toes dangled in the water have, so far, proved safe. A bone in the pike's head forms a cross and was worn as a preventative against witchcraft and epilepsy, the fat rubbed on the chests and soles of the feet of infants to prevent catarrh. As the Northern pike in America, it has several relations.

Catch The young haunt reedy shallows, rushing off as you wade. They are caught by spinning spoons or lures, often right on the surface in warm weather – deeper in the cold – or by dead baiting with herring or trolling the big lakes. Live baiting is allowed in Northern Ireland. Boated, snapping at your heels, in the middle of some wintry lough, water trickling down your neck, fingers numb with cold, the mind on a hot whiskey, this is a fish to remember. Kill one only, if you must.

Cook Skill is needed to fillet the pin- and y-shaped bones, but the white, sweet flesh is worth every effort. Preparing *quenelle de brochet* is too exhausting. Instead, for two, take a 2 lb (0.9 kg) pike and crimp (i.e. clean and scale, slash sides deeply and plunge in cold water for one hour). Simmer gently in heavily sea-salted water for 10 minutes. Keep warm. Make a roux with 1 oz (28 g) of butter, 1 oz flour, 1 tbsp cream, 1 tbsp water from the fish. Simmer for 10 minutes. Add a touch of cayenne, a dash of Worcester, a slice of lemon – and a dozen oysters or freshwater crayfish, if your fisherman can trap them.

Carp

Carp *Carbán* *Cyprinus carpio* Family: *Cyprinidae*

The majority of Europe's freshwater fish are members of the carp family, though the carp itself is quite localised in Ireland – roach, bronze bream, rudd and gudgeon being much more common. Other carp: barbel, asp, silver bream, bleak, bitterling, chub, goldfish, nase and ide, are entirely absent. Introduced to lakes on big estates (for example at Montalto or Castle Ward) as a food fish, the big, heavy carp are found in many shapes and sizes, as isolated groups take on various characteristics. Typically, the back is brown to brownish green, the sides golden; beneath, the skin is yellow. There are two pairs of barbels near the thick-lipped mouth and a bony ray at the front of the dorsal fin. Scales may be all over the fish, or greatly enlarged (mirror carp), or almost absent (leather carp). Typical fish are 7 lb (3 kg) and 20 in. (50 cm).

Catch There is an entire mystery and cult about carp-fishing. Specimen hunters have secret lakes and secret recipes for their curious baits of sweet-corn and luncheon meats, boiled together. Carbon rods and expensive reels accompany diaries noting water temperature and wind speed and light values, which are stashed in locked desks or computer files. Suffice it to say that carp prefer slow, warm, weedy water and spawn in mid-July. They bottom-feed for crustaceans, mid-water feed for plants and surface-feed for insects. Stealth, sharp hooks and soft lines are recommended. Very cunning and very cautious, carp usually live to a ripe old age. Ireland's best, 20 lb (9 kg), are caught in the Lough, Cork City.

Cook Common in *gefilte* fish, bred extensively in central and eastern Europe as a food fish and prized at Christmas, carp is a curiosity on Irish tables, though it is excellent hot-smoked when the big flaked flesh falls easily from the y-bones. Small fish should be scored, rubbed with a lemon, seasoned, grilled, basted frequently, then served on watercress.

Gudgeon *Brannóg* *Gobio Gobio* Family: *Cyprinidae*

Da. Grundling; *Du.* Grondel; *Fr.* Goujon; *Ge.* Gründling; *It.* Gobione; *Po.* Gobio; *Sp.* Gobio; *Sw.* Sandkrypare

This tiny, slim, silvery yellow-bellied fish, touched with darker tones of green dorsally and with a yellowish tinge to its sides, shoals gregariously on gravelly shallows in the middle reaches of rivers, where it spawns in early summer. The sticky blue eggs are shed at night. In winter it goes deeper. It will reach up to 6 in. (15 cm). A big fish would weigh 4 oz (113 g) and would feed on tiny freshwater shrimp. It is widespread across Europe, most of England, except Cornwall, and most of Ireland, except Galway, Mayo, Kerry and Cork. Thompson, the celebrated Irish naturalist, wrote of a dog who fed off them in the River Lagan. Dr Brookes, in a book referred to by Day only as *Hist. Fish 1772*, recommended them eaten live – considered good for a consumptive.

Catch This is a fish for picnic days down by a lazy river in the noonday sun. Walk the bank for the shade of a big oak or willow, or drift your clinker-built rowing boat to a mooring branch. Find your gravelly shallow, then rake the gravel with a stick, thus stirring the tiny creatures on which this charming little fish feeds. A tiny hook, the lightest of tackles, the smallest of bloodworm as bait will produce splendid fast sport. No need for float or sinker. The fish will bite from March to Michaelmas. Needless to say, they make excellent bait.

Cook Clean and wipe dry in the wind or summer sun. Construct a fire of sticks, if you have a pan, then fry in bubbling butter until crisp. Or score and grill. Hold in a napkin, munch whole as the sun dapples the grass. Consider the origin of the word *goujons*, a word which up to now you thought referred only to thin strips of sole or plaice rolled in seasoned flour and fried in unsalted butter until golden.

Tench *Cúramán Tinca tinca* Family: *Cyprinidae*

Da. Suder; *Du.* Zeelt; *Fr.* Tanche; *Ge.* Schlech, Schleie; *It.* Tinca; *No.* Suter; *Po.* Tenca; *Sp.* Tenca; *Sw.* Sutare; *We.* Gwrachen

This thick-set dark olive-coloured fish with strong spatulate pelvic and dorsal fins, orange-red eyes and a tiny pair of barbels, can grow up to around 7 lb (3.2 kg). Though the colour varies to golden with the location, the scales are so tiny you might think it had none, and the 'wrist' so thick, its slime so slimy, that the fish is unmistakable. A good fish would be 12 in. (30 cm). Its habitat is on the bottom of still or slow-flowing weedy, muddy waters near bulrushes. In the winter it can bury itself and hibernate. Though widely distributed and cultivated across Europe, in Ireland it is mostly confined to the Shannon basin. Tench were thought to cure sick fish; *cúram* means 'care' in Irish.

Catch The tench's ability to survive with little oxygen makes it easy to transfer to another water and to thrive as a sport-fish in poor-quality muddy water, so its range is spreading. It is caught mostly at summer dawn or dusk – or right through the summer night – making it suitable quarry (like carp) for obsessives. It is unkind to start a tench hunter talking about his hobby, as you will assuredly leave before he has well begun. Hooks, baits of bread flake, maggot or lobworm cast on a flowing trace will be part of his story. Spoil his day by noting that in Norfolk, tench were thought so dozy they were caught with bare hands.

Cook Abbeys fattened tench for the table. Dip into boiling water to aid descaling. Trim off the fins, gut, rub with salt. Place in acidulated water (2 tbsp vinegar; 1 tsp salt, 1¾pt or 1 litre water) to clear the muddy taste. Stuff with a mix of breadcrumbs, parsley, beaten eggs, bay leaf, sage, shallots, lemon juice, butter and seasoning. Bake in foil at 325°F (160°C) for one hour. Or bake for 25 minutes in a pre-heated oven with onions, shallots, garlic, parsley, a bouquet garni, oil, a bottle of dry cider or white wine, salt, pepper and saffron at 450°F (230°C).

Bream *Bran*, *Bréan Albramis brama* Family: *Cyprinidae*

Da. Brasen; *Du.* Brasem; *Fr.* Brême; *Ge.* Blei, Brachsen; *It.* Brama; *No.* Brasme; *Sw.* Braxen

This really is a slimy fish. Silver when small, bronze when larger, with a deep lozenge-shaped body and a distinctly forked tail, the bream's anal fin has more than twenty-five rays, which distinguishes it from the silver bream, which has less than twenty-five. Roach / bream hybrids are common and are more slimy, if that is possible. The common bream's fins are charcoal, the hybrid's redder, like those of the roach, and the body deeper. Rudd / bream hybrids also occur – they are distinguished by their smaller dorsal fins. The trouble with all these tests, though, is that you have to know your control is a pure-bred bream. Bream are distributed right across northern Europe, bar Celtic Wales, Scotland, Cornwall and Brittany. Despite this, they have spread across the midlands of central Ireland, as an early introduced species. The Irish record fish of 12 lb 3 oz was recorded in 1997 at Bolganard Lake.

Catch The best fish today are taken from Moynalty Lake, bottom-fishing with sweetcorn and maggots, but good, strong fish are taken right through the Shannon and Erne systems, where the heavy weight from the latter have aided a number of Five-Hour World Match records. Liberal ground baiting attracts the shoals, and steady, cautious topping up keeps the fish within ledgering range, using minimum shotting.

Cook As with most of this family of *Cyprinidae*, bream are esteemed and cultivated in parts of continental Europe, but distained in Ireland. They will hot-smoke well, the process freeing the flaky flesh from the y-bones. You can bravely wipe off the slime, trim the fins, de-scale, clean, soak in acidulated water (*see page 52*), then bake, braise, stuff or grill, using lots of strongly flavoured herbs – rosemary, for instance – plus shallots and bacon. Carp rules apply.

Minnow *Líbín, Pincín Phoxinus phoxinus* Family: *Cyprinidae*

Da. Elrits; *Du.* Elrits; *Fr.* Vairon; *Ge.* Elritze; *It.* Sanguinerola; *No.* Ørekyte; *Sp.* Piscardo; *Sw.* Kvidd; *We.* Bychan Byog

The smallest of the carp family, as its name declares from *minimus* – a tiny 5 in. (12.5 cm) fish – the minnow is olive green with a golden sheen fading to yellow on its belly and bars along its sides, giving it a striped appearance. Its dark spot on the 'wrist' is distinctive. The minnow is widespread in fast streams except in Donegal. In summer they will shoal at the foot of a ford, and if they are feeding from a single source can make wonderful flower-like patterns in clear water. They are rarely found near stream sources, presumably due to a lack of food.

Catch 'He is a sharp biter at a small worm, and in hot weather makes excellent sport for young anglers, or boys, or women that love that recreation,' said Izaak Walton (1593-1693), being sexist.
'Lay one when in full season on the palm of your hand, examine and admire him. Mark his beautiful colouring – every shade of olive, white, pale brown, silver, pink, and rosy harmoniously blended, producing that beautiful mottled appearance which reminds one of the Mackerel and of the *Salmo frontalis*, the lovely American Brook-trout,' noted the Rev. W. Houghton, quoting another enthusiast. To do this, first catch them with small hooks and small worms. They make excellent spinning bait for trout, perch and small pike.

Cook Once highly esteemed, a feature of state banquets in England and Scotland, minnows should be treated as whitebait (from unpolluted streams) or tossed in Izaak Walton's omelette, made with egg yolks, the flowers of cowslips and primroses, and a little tansy.

Rudd *Talóg, Ruán* *Scardinius erythrophthalmus* Family: *Cyprinidae*

Da. Rudskalle; *Du.* Ruisvoorn; *Fr.* Rotengle; *Ge.* Rotfeder; *It.* Scardola; *No.* Sørv; *Sw.* Sarv

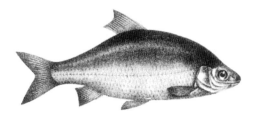

Common across northern continental Europe, southern England and all but the west coast of Ireland, the red-finned, silvery (when young), deep-bodied rudd favours still, weedy waters. When older, it grows darker, green backed and golden lustred. It differs from the roach by the fact that its iris is golden, its mouth points distinctly up (the roach's forward) and its dorsal fin starts well behind the pelvic. It grows to around 10 in. (25 cm). It spawns from April to June, feeds on insects and small fry and will go on feeding in the warm when most others have stopped.

Catch More a surface-feeder than the roach, rudd provide excellent sport from shaded summer lakesides, the wind dropped. In the warm silence, rudd are taken after surface ground-baiting with bread crusts on the lightest of shotting. A slow sinking maggot is effective, or a silver butcher fished wet-fly or a black gnat dry-fly fished. The Irish record stands at 4 lb 8 oz (2.17 kg).

Cook Farmed and fished commercially in eastern Europe, these pretty fish are not seen on menus or fishmongers' slabs in Ireland. Dip into boiling water, scale; trim fins and clean. Soak in acidulated water if the lake water was muddy. Coat whole fish – one or two per person – in flour and fry in clarified butter (butter which has been heated to frothing in a pan, then strained). Remove the fish. Keep it hot. Melt more butter, squeeze the juice of a lemon into it. Pour over the fish when serving. Add parsley. This is what chefs refer to as *à la meunière*. Day records that some thought the flesh of the rudd preferable to that of the roach. It is.

Carp

Dace *Déas Leuciscus leuciscus* Family: *Cyprinidae*

Da. Strømskalle; *Du*. Serpelling; *Fr*. Vandoise; *Ge*. Hasel; *No*. Gullbust; *Sw*. Stäm

The darting little dace, one of the most elegant of the carp family, is a quick silvery white-bellied fish, as gregarious as its better-known relative the roach. Dorsally it is blue green and it grows to 10 in. (25 cm) and 1.5 lb (680 g). It is a fish of clear, fast-flowing waters, but in Ireland is found in the Cork Blackwater and the River Barrow, where it was introduced. It spawns from February to May, occasionally ventures into lakes and is most frequently seen swarming on the surface in the warmer months. The dace will feed on algae and a number of water and terrestrial insects in the summer. In the winter the diet changes to tiny freshwater molluscs, leeches and crustacea.

Catch A truly excellent sport-fish due to their fine fighting qualities on light tackle, dace have been admired by anglers from Walton onwards, who recommended bread paste and also black flying ants as bait in summer, grubs in winter. Maggots and casters are now widely used and hemp seed will drive them daft at times. Wasp grubs are particularly effective when dace collect, as they do, in white-water pools. This method will, of course, secure any trout in the pool as well, which, considering the flavour of the dace, and providing you have permission to catch the trout, would be a bonus for the cook-angler. A floating line and dark nymphs will work well for the fly-fisher, or alternatively a sinking nymph. In winter dace are tempted from under bank hollows and tree roots with maggot.

Cook Dace are small and are not sought primarily as a food fish, the flesh being soft and rather full of bones. However, they can be eaten and are best between September and October, fried *à la meunière* (see page 55) after cleaning, drying and being rolled in seasoned flour.

Roach *Róiste Rutilus rutilus* Family: *Cyprinidae*

Da. Skalle; *Du*. Blankvoorn; *Fr*. Gardon; *Ge*. Plötze, Rotauge; *It*. Triotto; *No*. Mort; *Sp*. Bermejulea; *Sw*. Mört

Roach is the most common of fish in lowland waters in much of northern Europe – except Brittany, Scotland, Wales and Cornwall – as well as Ireland, where it is gradually spreading across the midlands since its original introduction. Deep bodied and silvery, with red fins and a red iris to the eye, the roach is gradually replacing the rudd in the Erne, Foyle and Cork Blackwater, colonising everywhere. According to K'eogh (*see Bibliography*): 'the gall is useful to be applied to sore eyes, being mixt with honey: Roches afford good nourishment being easily digested, they provoke lust, and help cure fevers.'

Catch Walton referred to roach contemptuously as 'water sheep', and Dame Juliana Berniers, Prioress of Sopewell Nunnery, noted in the fifteenth-century *Boke of St Albans* that 'the roche is an easy fysshe to take'. And so they are if you only want a few; then they will respond easily to maggot and worm. The world of competitive match-anglers is galaxies away from this, where the lightest of tackle, the smallest of hooks and years of acquired skill have led to, for instance, 100 lb (45.35 kg) keep-nets on the Erne, the Bann and the Shannon. Women who have encountered match-anglers in the bar after a hard Five-Hour Match can attest to the accuracy of the penultimate part of K'eogh's observation. The Irish record, from Drumacritten Lake, weighed 1.425 kg.

Cook Day considers roach to be coarse and flabby, but at their best in October from a gravelly, clean stream (true of all freshwater fish) and baked in intermediate layers, with bay leaves and a little spice. Scaled, de-gilled, trimmed, cleaned, rubbed with salt, soaked in acidulated water, they should be fried *à la meunière* as rudd (*see page 55*), the fillets cut in thin strips, rolled in seasoned flour and fried in butter.

Stone Loach *Cailleach rua Noemacheilus barbatulus* Family: *Cobitidae*

Da. Smerling; *Du.* Bermpje; *Fr.* Loche Franche; *Ge.* Schmerle; *It.* Cobite Barbatello; *Sp.* Pez Lobo; *Sw.* Grönling

Growing not above a finger long and no thicker than is suitable to that length, the Irish loach, with its elongated, mottled olive-green body, three distinct pairs of barbels and square-cut tail, is unlikely to be confused with anything else. The skin is quite slimy. The Irish name means 'old woman'. The spined loach, or groundling, never made it to Ireland, and the related weatherfish, *Misgurnus fossilis*, is confined to continental Europe. Stone loach grow to 5 in. (12.5 cm) in clear streams and along the shorelines of lakes. Under stones during the day, the loach comes out at night or on dull days to forage and feed on bottom-living invertebrates. It is sensitive to pollution and is thus a useful indicator of water quality.

Catch 'He is to be fished for with a very small worm, at the bottom for he very seldom, or never, rises above the gravel' – Walton again. This, the only Irish loach, is caught in jam jars by kids.

Cook Walton thought stone loach a most dainty fish. Yarrell reported that in some parts of Europe it was considered an exquisite delicacy, so much so that there was a practice of transporting loach to streams on the estates of the wealthy. Frederick I of Sweden was one such landowner. Some authorities in the past recommended loach for an invalid's diet. Sporting gentlemen, it has been reported, would toss back a live loach in a generous glass of wine as a frolic. It can be preserved in the manner of anchovies and mushed, then cooked by sautéing into a paste. Much simpler, though, to wash, dry, flour, then grill or fry.

Eel

Eel *Eascann* *Anguilla anguilla* Family: *Anguillidae*

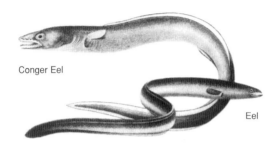

Conger Eel

Eel

Delicacies to the Greeks, gods to the Egyptians, despised by the Romans, forbidden to the Jews, eels are amongst the most prolific fish. Spawned in the Sargasso Sea, they drift on the Gulf Stream and Atlantic Drift, taking three years to reach Ireland's shores, metamorphosing into elvers, about $2\frac{3}{4}$ in. (7 cm) long when they get here. Some stay in estuaries, maturing, but most go up-river turning from transparent to black, the rivers turning black, too, from their numbers. In lakes such as Lough Neagh they feed from seven to fifteen years, brown-or yellow-bellied, devouring everything they can. Some will wriggle overland, on wet and dewy nights, to other waters. In autumn, on a wet and moonless night, they turn for the sea again to spawn, their bellies going silver, their eyes bright blue, protruding. Four thousand miles and eighteen months away lies the Sargasso from which they came, and in which they will die. *Anguilla rosata*, *Anguilla australis* and *Anguilla japonica* are related species. K'eogh (*see Bibliography*) quotes the liver and gall of eels, being powdered and taken with wine, as without equal for hastening labour. Its fat he recommends for mitigating the pain of haemorrhoids; dropped in the ears, it aids hearing.

Catch Eels are caught with an unweighted dead bait; the bigger the bait, the bigger the eel – within reason. An oily, bloody bait is best. If it is a big bait, let the eel have one free run before you strike. Most, though, are caught commercially. Lough Neagh is the biggest eel fishery in Europe. The tradition continues in other lakes.

Eel

Cook Little eel appears on Irish menus (except in good Chinese or Japanese restaurants) or on marble slabs, except that which has flown to the Netherlands to be smoked and brought back to be eaten with wheaten bread, good butter, a slice of lemon and parsley. Catch them, or buy the rare few. Clean, marinate for 6 hours with chunks of smokey bacon in oil, salt, pepper, lemon segments, parsley and thyme. Cut into 2 in. (5 cm) lengths, skewer alternately with bacon. Barbecue, brushing with the marinade. Elvers dropped in seasoned boiling oil are magic.

Conger Eel *Eascann mara, Eascann choncair* *Conger conger*
Family: *Congridae*

Am. American Conger*; *Da.* Havål; *Du.* Kongeraal, Zeepaling; *Fr.* Congre; *Ge.* Meeraal; *It.* Grongo; *No.* Havål; *Po.* Congro; *Sp.* Cóngrio; *Sw.* Havsål; *We.* Môr-Lysywen

The eel grows to 10 lb (4.5 kg); the eastern Atlantic/Mediterranean conger to 100 lb. The conger stays at sea, its leaden-to-blackish heavy, muscular body is stouter. Its dorsal fin begins almost level with its pectorals, whereas in the eel there is a large gap. The conger lives on rough ground offshore and close in, particularly in and around harbours and estuaries. Sexually ripe conger have never been seen. If kept in tanks, fish approaching ripeness decay, losing teeth, decalcifying, dying. All that is known is that spawning takes place in mid-water in mid-summer, between Gibraltar and the Azores, after which the young make their way back, like the eel, metamorphosing as they approach shore. In past times the skins were dried and used as leather for the hingeing of flails. The western Atlantic conger*, *conger oceanicus*, is closely related.

Catch Conger will take most baits, feeding best on warm, muggy summer nights with the freshest of temptations. They are taken from boats, from harbour walls, from dark cliffs, and from holes in the deepest of wrecks. Boated, they are an awesome sight: malevolent – so it seems – of eye, brutal, the jaws closing even after death. Caution and a good skipper are well advised. Dacron line on a 50 lb (22.5 kg) outfit, 80 lb (36 kg) terminal monofilament, 100 lb (45 kg) wire trace on a Clement's boom, a 6/0 hook and you are in for some exacting sport. Once a bite is felt, tempt the beast from its holt before you strike. Use a gaff to boat it. Kill with a severe blow on the back with the heaviest priest available.

Cook Cut into steaks. Steam, then fry in dripping. Or casserole the steaks under a layer of potatoes and onions, half covered in milk – or with onion, thyme, parsley, bay leaves, salt and pepper, garlic, and stout or red wine.

Garfish

Garfish *Corr uaine, Ronnagh Spáinneach*** *Belone belone* Family: *Belonidae*

Am. Needlefish*; *Da*. Hornfisk; *Du*. Geep; *Fr*. Orphie; *Ge*. Hornhecht; *It*. Aguglia; *Po*. Agulha; *No*. Horngjel; *Sp*. Aguja; *Sw*. Hornfisk; *We*. Môr Nodwydd

Confusingly translated as Spanish mackerel** in Irish, the garfish is no relation to the members of the mackerel family (*see page 94*). All the members of the *Belone* family, east and west of the Atlantic and in the Pacific, are distinguished by their long, slender bodies and startlingly vivid green bones. True, this voracious fish hunts ahead of the mackerel shoals and has a brilliant bluey-green back and silver sides reminiscent of the mackerel's. In summer waters they jump like flying fish, as do the aptly named skipper or saury pike, also illustrated, looking like a fat garfish with a long silver stripe. Assorted *Syngnathidae* – *Snáithaid mhara* in Irish – the pipe-cleaner shaped pipefish and sea-horses, dried, are sold as curios.

Catch While the garfish you will catch will rarely exceed 1.5 lb (600 g), catching them off the rocks in late warm summer – the fresh spume on your face, terns diving for fry out to sea, waves crashing white, blue and green below you – is the stuff of magic. A trout spinning-rod with just a 3 lb (1.35 kg) line and a silver condor bait would be perfect. Come back at dawn or dusk if the fry are in close, this time with a fly-rod, a sinking line and a homemade fly. Take a number 6-long shanked hook, wrap in silver paper, tie on a bunch of white stripped from a tern's feather lying on the rocks, or a bishop's robe-coloured fuchsia flower from which you've first sucked the nectar. Take a child with you; they'll fish forever afterwards.

Cook Many cannot face the viridian colour of the bones. So perhaps, if you can, don't reveal the fillet's source when, after removing them gently from the quickly hidden bones, you roll the strips up, secure with a wooden cocktail stick, marinate in seasoned oil and then grill.

Garfish

Garfish

Skipper / Saury Pike

Sea-horse

Codfish

Whiting *Faotín Merlangius merlangus* Family: *Gadidae*

Am. Silver Hake*; *Da.* Hvitting; *Du.* Wijting; *Fr.* Merlan; *Ge.* Wittling; *No.* Kviting; *Po.* Badejo; *Sp.* Merlán; *Sw.* Vitling; *We.* Gwyniad y Môr

A pinky brown above, silvery along the sides and alone amongst the cod family in having no barbels, a big whiting would weigh in at 3 lb (1.36 kg), 12 in. (30 cm) in length. There is a dark spot just in front of the pectorals. The upper jaw is much longer than the lower. It ranges widely round the eastern Atlantic coastline, and huge shoals were once a common feature of both commercial and sport-fishing off Ireland, particularly over sandy shallows. The related blue whiting, *Micromesistius poutassou – faotín gorm* in Irish – with no pre-pectoral spot, a deep-water fish, is blue not brown. The silver hake, *Merluccius bilinearis*, is called whiting, too.

Catch The whiting are splendid feeders in broad daylight, but when they arrive in shoals, and you are engaged in boat-fishing, they can make for a boring day, as it becomes impossible to get a bait down past them. However, due to more intense fishing of late, chances of such boredom are a thing of the past. The Victorians delighted in whiffing for whiting – trolling a line slowly – particularly in rough weather when keeping the boat under way also made for more comfortable fishing. Sadly, the whiting's fighting abilities do not match its appetite.

Cook The flesh is delicately flavoured and white, but the stigma of being served, poached, as a dish for the delicately stomached has put it into unnecessary disfavour. Split and dress one small whiting per person. Season. Brush with melted butter. Grill, basting with butter. Serve sprinkled with parsley. Better still, remove the backbone, dip first in seasoned wholemeal flour, then in egg beaten in milk, then in oatmeal or porridge oats. Deep-fry, drain on kitchen paper and serve with a homemade tartare sauce – or bought, if you're lazy.

Pouting / Bib / Pout Saraoilleog, Praiscin, Trosgán stopóige Trisopterus luscus
Family: Gadidae

Da. Skaegtorsk; Du. Steenbolk; Fr. Tacaud; Ge. Franzosendorch; It. Merluzzo
Francese; No. Skjeggtorsk; Sp. Faneca

Pink to bronze, the darker colour in bands when freshly caught, and with a black
spot at the base of the pectoral fins (brighter than the whiting and deeper in the
body), the pouting, pout or bib can also be distinguished from the whiting by
having a long wispy barbel, or bib, under the chin. It is distinguished from the
poor cod by having its first anal fin starting mid-way under the first dorsal fin.

Poor Cod Trosgán Trisopterus minutus

Da. Glyse; Du. Dwergbolk; Fr. Capelan; Ge. Zwergdorsch; It. Merluzzo
Cappellano; No. Sypike; Po. Fanecào, Sp. Mollera; Sw. Glyskoljal

In the poor cod the first anal fin begins directly below the start of the second
dorsal.

Norway Pout Trosgán Ioruach Trisopterus esmarkii

Da. Spærling; Fr. Tacaud Norvégien; Ge. Spärling; No. Øyenpåle

This is a slim version of the poor cod. Common around the coasts, the young
enter estuaries in summer. It reaches a length of 12 in. (30 cm) when it might
weigh almost 3 lb (1.36 kg), but usually it weighs much less.

Catch Though frequently caught, pouting are rarely sought after and
unfortunately have but a brief moment, literally, of glory when they are caught.
Then they look dazzling, but the colours quickly fade and most anglers treat
them as a nuisance, taking bait intended for bigger fish, either when casting from
the shore with lugworm for cod, or when boat-fishing with rag and mackerel strip.
Still, on an otherwise blank day, they may break the duck which is giving your
fellow anglers opportunities to scoff. It prefers rough ground and feeds better at
dusk.

Cook More bony than the whiting and saddled with flesh which goes soft and
spoils rapidly, pouting must, if kept for the pot, be placed well out of the sun till
the boat docks or the tackle is packed. If it is all you come back with, don't
despair. Prepare it quickly. Fry the fillets.

Pouting

Poor Cod

Blue Whiting

Codfish

Pollack *Mangach* *Pollachius pollachius* Family: *Gadidae*

Da. Lubbe; *Du.* Pollak; *Fr.* Colin, Lieu Jaune; *Ge.* Pollack; *It.* Merluzzo Giallo; *No.* Lyr; *Po.* Juliana; *Sp.* Abadejo; *Sw.* Bleka

Pollack and coalfish are often confused. Pollack, or lythe, have a brown bronze-green back. The coalfish's, blockan's or saithe's is dark green to black – hence the name. The pollack's tail is not forked; the coalfish's is. The pollack's lateral line is bent, the coalfish's is almost straight. Pollack grow to 20 lb (9 kg), big coalfish and greylords to twice that. Small coleys are called gilpins. Unlike coalfish, Pollack are only found in the eastern, not western Atlantic.

Catch In autumn an underwater gulley in a rough, rocked peninsula – spun or trolled over slowly towards dusk on an incoming tide, with just a single red rubber eel – can produce huge fish. The biggest, though, can be taken just off the edge of deep undersea pinnacles at the turn of strong autumn tides.

Cook Prepare and cook as for cod (*see page 68*).

Coalfish *Glasán*, *Blocán* *Pollachius virens*

Am. Pollock; *Da.* Sej; *Du.* Koolvis; *Fr.* Lieu Noir; *Ge.* Köhler; *It.* Merluzzo Nero; *No.* Sei; *Sp.* Carbonero; *Sw.* Sej

Cod *Trosc* *Gadus morhua* Family: *Gadidae*

Am. Atlantic Cod, Scrod; *Da.* Torsk; *Du.* Kabeljauw, Cul; *Fr.* Cabillaud, Morue; *Ge.* Kabeljau, Dorsch; *It.* Merluzzo Bianco; *No.* Torsk, Skrei; *Po.* Bacalhau; *Sp.* Bacalao; *Sw.* Torsk; *We.* Penfras

Cod, the mainstay of so much commercial fishing, make their way south to spawn, from February to April, and the young then eat their way back north again. There is uncertainty as to whether they can be divided into separate races depending on their location. In general, they are recognised by the three dorsal and two anal well-rounded fins and their long barbels. Back colour varies from sandy brown with a greenish tinge, and pale green, to burnished reddy brown – all these colours variously mottled. Some describe the commonest colour as Connemara marble. The upper jaw protrudes; the lateral line, in adults, is white. They can grow to over 100 lb (45 kg), but the Irish record line-caught fish weighed in at 42 lb (19 kg).

Pollack

Coalfish

Cod

Codfish

Catch Cod can be taken on mackerel feathers right round the Irish coast, but the biggest seem to be taken consistently out of Ballycotton. Beach-fishing at night, after a storm, with bunches of lugworm or razorfish, on a simple paternoster rig with a breakaway lead, has much to recommend it at the evening flood – tilley lamps primed, hot coffee flask stiffened with a half 'un of whiskey. Boat-fishing with ledgered baits of lug and squid and 30 lb (13.5 kg) gear is good sport. Pirking with heavy chromed pirks is for the strong armed. Live baiting with small whiting, on a brace of sequential hooks, will work from beach or boat if you have no scruples about it. Red gill eels can also be profitable.

Cook The cod's fine flesh can be cooked in any manner you fancy – fry, steam, poach or bake. Small codling baked with potatoes and mussels, onions, thyme, salt and pepper, parsley and butter in a hot oven (430°F / 220°C) are really hard to beat.

Haddock *Cadóg Melanogrammus aeglifinus* Family: *Gadidae*

Am. Scrod; *Da*. Kuller; *Du*. Schelvis; *Fr*. Eglefin; *Ge*. Schellfisch; *It*. Asinello; *No*. Hyse; *Sp*. Eglefino; *We*. Corbenfras

In no way related to the two rare vermillion-coloured Norway haddocks, *Sebastes viviparus* and *Sebastes marinus*, and the blue mouth, *Helicolenus dactylopterus*, and the related delicious fish the French call *rascasses*, this greyish-green fish is easily distinguished by the conspicuous thumb-print (like the John Dory's) on its shoulder. Haddock grow to over 10 lb (4.54 kg), length around 20 in. (50 cm), and indeed the Irish record fish, caught off Kinsale, weighed 10 lb 13.5 oz. They are fished commercially from Brittany to Newfoundland, and over 4,000 tonnes are landed by Irish boats in a good year. Scrod is American for the young.

Torsk *Brosme brosme*

Du. Lom; *Fr*. Brosme; *Ge*. Lumb; *It*. Brosmio; *Sp*. Brosmio

Looking slightly like a shortened ling, the torsk, a fish of northern waters, has a single long dorsal fin running right back till it joins the anal fin at its base. Grey to brown it grows to 43 in. (108 cm).

Haddock

Torsk

Norway Haddock *Cadóg Ioruach Sebastes viviparus* Family: *Gadidae*

Da. Lille Rødfish; *Ge*. Kleiner Rotbarsch; *No*. Berggalt

This is the smallest of the 'red-fish' found in the waters off the north coast, growing only to 10 in. (25 cm). It comes further inshore than the rest of the family, which are beginning to be part of an expanding fishery.

Catch Though haddock do not come high on the sea-angler's list, they are very good to eat. Bottom-feeders, they take worm readily, but stocks fluctuate wildly, being readily available for a while and then disappearing. Methods of catch can be versions of those used for cod, though paternostering slim little silver spoons, actually called haddock spoons, each with an integral hook, would seem the logical way.

Cook It is the little village of Finnan, near Aberdeen, with which the haddock, soaked in brine and cooked over peat (turf) smoke, is associated worldwide, sold as Finnan haddie. Bake fillets of the smoked fish in a closed buttered dish, covered with a layer of smoked bacon. Remove the lid to crisp the bacon before serving. Even better is a chowder called, wonderfully, cullen skink, made first by simmering a Finnan with a little water and chopped onion till the flesh goes creamy. Remove; flake off the flesh. Simmer the bones to make a stock. Strain. Boil again and add 1 pt (0.5 litre) boiling milk and the flaked fish. Simmer for a few minutes, adding mashed potato to taste plus $\frac{1}{2}$ oz (15 g) butter and seasoning, then a spoonful of cream and chopped parsley as you serve.

Hake *Colmóir Merluccius merluccius* Family: *Gadidae*

Da. Kolmuller; *Du*. Heek; *Fr*. Merlu; *Ge*. Sechechte; *It*. Nasello; *No*. Haeg; *Po*. Pescada; *Sp*. Merluza; *Sw*. Kummel; *We*. Ceggdu

A slate-grey fish which runs up to about a metre long, the hake has dangerous looking teeth, a noticeably black inside to its mouth and no barbel. The lateral line is absolutely straight. Over 1,000 tonnes are landed annually in Irish waters, but it is the Portuguese who regard this fish as the best of all. The Irish record fish weighed 25 lb 5.5 oz (11.5 kg), caught in Belfast Lough in 1962. The slightly smaller silver hake, *Merluccius bilinearis*, iridescent when fresh and with a blue mouth, is caught in the western Atlantic and also makes excellent eating. Two other western Atlantic fish called *Urophycis chuss* and *Urophysis tenuis* are not so closely related.

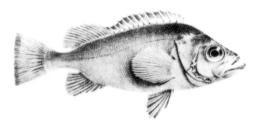

Norway Haddock

Hake

Catch A voracious night feeder, the hake comes inshore after small fish and fry, and, on the west coast, the season really begins in September. Those prepared to brave the Atlantic storms might catch more later in the year. Most methods used for cod will catch hake if they are about, but a sliver of mackerel near the bottom in mid-water at dusk is always to be recommended.

Cook A favourite food in Portugal and Spain's Galicia, hake has much to recommend it. Though often sold in fillets it is better flavoured when cooked as steaks, either simply grilled under a very hot grill or on a hot griddle after suitable marinating. Alternatively, bake in a moderate oven as follows: put a layer of hake steaks in a buttered dish, splash with lemon juice, season, cover with a layer of sliced, parboiled potatoes, then do the same again. Cover with a white sauce perked with grated nutmeg. Even better, marinate shredded hake fillets in a mix of best olive oil and sherry vinegar (3 to 1), flavoured with a handful of green peppercorns and parsley for 48 hours. Drain. Serve tossed with green salad.

Ling *Langa* *Molva molva* Family: *Gadidae*

Da. Lange; *Du*. Leng; *Fr*. Lingue, Julienne; *Ge*. Leng; *It*. Molva; *No*. Lange; *Po*. Juliana; *Sp*. Maruca; *Sw*. Langa; *We*. Honos

Almost eel-like in appearance, the back a mottled, marbled bronze green, the skin slimy, the ling, with its pronounced barbel, is quite distinctive. It can run up to a metre long and up to 50 lb (22.5 kg) in weight. Distribution is widespread. The unrelated American ling, or cobia, is a member of the *Rachycentridae*.

Spanish Ling *Langa Spáinneach* *Molva macrophthalma*

A ling with a protruding lower jaw and pelvic (ventral) fins reaching past the pectorals, body elongated.

Blue Ling *Langa gorm* *Molva dypterygia*

A rare ling with a protruding lower jaw and pelvic fins not reaching past the pectorals.

Ling

Three-bearded Rockling

Four-bearded Rockling

Five-bearded Rockling

Tadpole Fish

Three-Bearded Rockling *Langa carraige* *Gaidropsaurus vulgaris*

Da. Tretrådet Havkvabbe; *Du.* Dreidradge Meun; *Fr.* Motelle à Trois Barbillons; *Ge.* Dreibärtelige Seequappe; *No.* Tretrådet Tangbrosme; *Po.* Laibeque; *Sp.* Lota; *Sw.* Tretömmad Skårlånga

This fish, which grows up to 21 in. (53 cm), is salmon pink with brown blotching. It looks like a small (up to 2 lb/0.9 kg) reddish ling with an extra two barbels. The rocklings, which have assorted numbers of barbels are illustrated opposite. The four-bearded rockling, which grows up to 16 in. (40 cm), is reddish brown dorsally, with a grey-blue belly and a round black spot at the rear end of the second dorsal and anal fins. The five-bearded rockling grows to just 8 in. (20 cm) and is dark brown.

Tadpole Fish / Lesser Fork-Beard *Donnánach dubh* *Raniceps rannius*

Du. Vorschkwal; *Fr.* Trident; *Ge.* Froschdorsch; *No.* Paddetorsk

Another related dark-brown, small (10 in./25 cm) fish with a single barbel. The greater fork-beard, over twice the size and lighter in colour, is possibly more common.

Catch Ling are taken near wrecks or over the edge of deep chasms. Day quotes big fish taken in Irish waters, one was found with a pewter flask containing two glasses of ardent spirit, and another had a three-gill bottle in the stomach. Perhaps marinate your bait in whiskey?

Cook Cook as cod or cut your shop-bought, traditionally salted ling into suitably sized portions and soak overnight in a half-and-half mixture of milk and water seasoned with sliced onion. Bring the lot to the boil. Cook. Remove the fish. Keep hot. Thicken the liquid with flour to make the necessary sauce. Serve with champ: soak potatoes in cold water for an hour, add salt, boil until well cooked. Drain and drape a folded tea towel over the pot whilst keeping hot for 5 minutes – it makes the spuds floury. Mash with chopped chives or scallion, a dash of milk (buttermilk is better) and a big knob of butter. Flour and fry the rocklings.

Dory

John Dory *Donnchad na súl mór, leathóg Dé, Deorai Zeus faber*
Family: *Zeidae*

Da. Sankt Peters-Fisk; *Du.* Zonnevis; *Fr.* St Pierre; *Ge.* Heringskönig; *It.* Pesce San Pietro; *No.* St Peterfisk; *Po.* Peixe São Pedro; *Sp.* Pez de San Pedro; *Sw.* Sankt Pers Fisk; *We.* Sion Dori.

This splendidly baroque-looking fish may owe its name to the legend that St Peter is said to have picked it up to obtain tribute money, leaving his thumb prints ringed in faint gold. Others say the John Dory comes from the French *jaune dorée* (golden yellow), its colour when fresh. More likely, it may be a corruption of the Italian *janitore* (janitor), and of course St Peter was the keeper of the keys. It is a solitary, voracious fish as its massive jaws testify. The Dory stalks its prey, then chomps. It can grow up to 8 lb (3.63 kg), the female fish being the bigger, running up to 25 in. (63 cm). Males grow to two thirds of this measure. The tiny 6 in. (15 cm) related boar-fish, *Capros aper*, varies from red to yellow.

Catch Not frequent enough in Irish waters to be sought after, the Dory will take most fish-strip and used to be caught on small, live fish. Care must be taken when handling a wriggling Dory as the spines can inflict very painful injuries, especially around the finger joints. Grasp the fish firmly, collapsing the fins forcibly. As to tactics – the fish is said to swim leaning over to one side, if that helps, and it is caught off rocky western shores.

Dory

Cook With its vast mouth and head and fine fins, there isn't a great deal of flesh on a Dory, but what there is, is delicious. Clean, de-gill, trim, scale, then poach whole fish on the bone gently in cider, dry wine or a light beer, or in the court-bouillon of your choice. Lift back the skin when cooked and the fillets are easily served. The head and bones will later make excellent stock. Or perhaps you may prefer fillets fried or treated like the flesh of any of the flatfish. Another fine method is to slash the flesh, place slices of lemon in the cuts and bake. Or steam, gently, on a bed of bladder wrack.

Bass

Bass *Doingean, Bas Dicentrarchus labrax*
Family: *Percichthyidae*

Am. European Sea Bass; *Da*. Bars; *Du*. Zeebars; *Fr*. Bar Loup; *Ge*. Seebarch; *It*.
Spigola; *No*. Hav-àbor; *Po*. Robalo; *Sp*. Lubina; *Sw*. Havsabborre

Powerful, slim, silvery sided, with its bluey-grey back and gold-tinged belly, bass
is distinguished by its separate large-spined first dorsal fin, fierce forward-
pointing teeth on the inside of the cheek bone, hard scales, and the diffuse dark
spot on the edge of the gill cover. A good fish would be 10 lb (4.54 kg). The young
may be spotted, but large, spotted specimens are the spotted sea bass,
Dicentrarchus punctatus. Its distribution is mainly off the south and west coasts
of Ireland. There are several American species, but it is sadly worth noting that
America's favourite, the striped bass, is unavailable due to unacceptably high
levels of PCBs.

Stone Basse/Wreckfish *Breac giúirlinne Polyprion americanus*

Da. Vragfisk; *Du*. Wrakbaars; *Fr*. Cernier; *Ge*. Wrackbarsch; *It*. Cernia di
Fondale; *Po*. Cherne; *Sp*. Cherna

Rare and fatter and with two dorsals which are continuous, it has drab, blotchy
colouring and grows to 80 in. (200 cm). The wreckfish's name comes from its
habit of following floating seaweed or ships' wreckage.

Stone Basse / Wreckfish

Comber *Cíoradóir Serranus cabrilla* Family: *Serranidae*

Fr. Serran; *Ge*. Sägebarsch; *It*. Percia; *Po*. Alecrim; *Sp*. Cabrilla

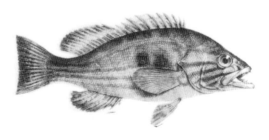

Similar in outline, but with dramatic chocolate-dark dorsal bars and green streaks, the comber grows to 10 in. (25 cm).

Dusky Perch / Grouper *Crónbhui Epinephelus guaza*

Fr. Mérou; *It.* Cernia; *Sp.* Mero

This delicious Mediterranean *mérou*, a rather similar chocolate-brown fish running to 36 in. (90cm), was taken off Galway twice in the twentieth century.

Catch Winter beach-fishing for bass on long wind-smashed Kerry beaches is one of Ireland's sporting delights, despite diminishing stocks. They can also be caught float-fishing off rocks, spun for in estuaries, even fly-fished when they are running after whitebait. Beach gear is an 11 ft (3.35 m) rod, small multiplier, 10 lb (4.5 kg) line, single hook tied paternoster fashion and lug, rag, razorfish – or squid for bigger fish.

Cook It is the fashion to call these fish sea bass (absurd, since we have no freshwater bass), but order it nevertheless when you see it. Poach bass steaks in a court-bouillon. Poach chopped shallots in 4 tbsp wine vinegar and 2 tbsp court-bouillon. Season. Reduce. Add 1 lb (500 g) butter slowly, beating as you go. Add 1 tbsp cream. Serve over the steaks.

Perch

Perch *Péirse* *Perca fluviatilis* Family: *Percidae*

The only member of the perch family found in Ireland (no ruffe nor pope nor zander here), this beautiful fish is widely distributed right across north-western Europe, apart from much of Scotland. Its back is greenish brown crossed by dark bars, the sides yellow, the belly white. The pelvic, anal and tail fins are red to orange. There is a dark spot at the rear of the spiny first dorsal. An Irish record fish, caught in the Erne, weighed 5.8 lb (2.50 kg) and would have measured around 20 in. (50 cm). The American yellow perch, *Perca flavescens*, is closely related, the sauger and the walleye not so closely. The perch is found in rivers, streams and lakes and when mature will eat sticklebacks, roach and perch fry, water boatmen, damselfly nymphs and water slaters. K'eogh (*see Bibliography*) recommended stones from the head to be ground and used as a dentifrice.

Catch Perch are predatory fish, lying in wait under overhanging branches and fallen tree trunks. They will take most bait – worms, grubs, bread, insects and freshwater shellfish. Should you seek out the landscape's natural baits, this will add a lot to your enjoyment of the countryside. Otherwise, spinning with a small Mepps, or fly-fishing with a long silver fly could not be bettered.

Cook I have eaten perch both grilled by an open river-bank fire, the fish spiked on a stick like a lollipop, and hot smoked by a lakeside and found them excellent, the white flesh falling easily from the bones. At home, pre-heat a moderate oven. Make a white roux with 1 oz (28 g) each of butter and flour over low heat. Blend in 1 fl oz of both milk and fish stock. Add $\frac{1}{2}$pt (250 mls) of fresh cream. Season with salt, pepper and nutmeg. Cook for 20 minutes. Range the perch fillets on a bed of this sauce in a buttered dish. Cover with more, plus 2 oz (57 g) of melted butter. Bake.

Scad

Scad/Horse Mackerel *Scadán carraige, Gabhar, Bolmán Trachurus trachurus*
Family: *Carangidae*

Am. Jenny Lind; *Da.* Hestemakrel; *Du.* Horsmakreel; *Fr.* Chinchard, Saurel; *Ge.* Bastardmakrele; *It.* Suro; *No.* Taggmakrell; *Po.* Carapau; *Sp.* Chincharro, Jurele; *Sw.* Taggmakrill

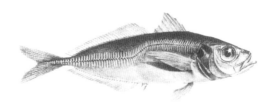

The scad's distinguishing feature is the conspicuous line of keeled plates – looking a bit like a zip – running along each side following the lateral line. There is a diffused dark spot on the operculum or gill cover. The colour is blue to green above, the sides steel blue. The belly is sometimes of an odd yellowish tinge. It has a mackerel shape about it and can grow to 3 lb (1.36 kg), though the Irish record is just under 2 lb (0.9 kg). Its range runs from Portugal to the Baltic and to the western Atlantic, and it has an American relative called, for obvious reasons, the goggle-eyed scad. One of its names in Irish, *gabhar*, means goat.

Of the other members of this family, a rare specimen of the bluish pilot-fish, *Nuacrates ductor* – *píolóta* in Irish – which can grow to 12 in. (30 cm) and which has three to five strong spines in front of the dorsal fin and a lateral, fleshy keel on the sides towards the tail, is sometimes taken off the south west. The names come from its habit of journeying in the company of sharks, whales and boats. The even rarer derbio, *Trachinotus ovatus*, blue backed, yellow sided, silvery-pink bellied, and with a row of lateral spots, can grow to 16 in. (40 cm) and is also a southern wanderer, taken once off the north-east coast.

Catch It is doubtful if sport-anglers ever set out by boat purely to catch scad, but they are a hungry fish which will take any bait offered and often run in huge shoals in the autumn, chasing fry, particularly around the Donegal and Antrim coasts. They are in turn pursued by Japanese factory ships.

Pilot-Fish

Derbio

Ray's Bream

Ray's Bream *Sáimhín Brama brama* Family: *Bramidae*

Am. Atlantic Pomfret; *Da*. Havbrasen; *Du*. Braam; *Fr*. Brème de Mer, Castagnole;
Ge. Brachsenmakrele; *It*. Pesce Castanga; *No*. Havbrasme; *Po*. Chaputa, Friera;
Sp. Palometa, Japuta; *Sw*. Rays Havbrax

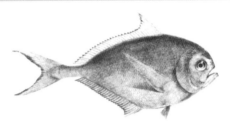

Common and prized from the deep waters off northern Portugal, Ray's bream
swims north in warm autumns and is caught off the south west, where its startling
black to silvery gun-metal grey appearance surprises many an angler. It can be up
to 27 in. (70 cm). It has a single dorsal and single anal fin, a deeply compressed
body and a marvellous crescent tail. It feeds on small fish and squid. The bream's
name comes from the first naturalist to record a fair description, having obtained a
washed-up dead specimen at the mouth of the Yorkshire Tees on 18 September
1681. This specimen later came into the possession of Dr Johnson. A specimen
taken off Tramore in October 1843 was presented by a Dr Burkitt of Waterford to
Trinity College. North America also has bigscale and Pacific pomfrets, but neither
the Mediterranean pomfret, *Stromateus fiatola*, nor the delicious pomfrets (also
from the family *Stromateidae* – butterfish) eaten from Bombay to Bangkok, are
related.

Catch Not to be confused with the black sea bream, the Ray's bream will be
caught, probably by accident, on a warm autumn day after a period of northwards-
driving storms, with a bait of squid strip.

Cook If this was not a book of Irish fish, the author would have suggested that you
marinate whole fish in a mixture of coconut cream, onions, garlic, lemon juice and
strong black pepper for several hours before grilling over charcoal, basting with the
marinade. But since this is an Irish book, let us poach the fish in a court-bouillon,
browning it under the grill before serving. Otherwise, score the fish, cram the cuts
with fresh rosemary and fennel, leave to marinate, then bake in a well-buttered
dish with generous slices of lemon and tomato.

Red Mullet

Red Mullet *Milléad dearg* *Mullus surmuletus* Family: *Mullidae*

Am. Goatfish*; *Da.* Mulle; *Du.* Mul, Zee Barbeel; *Fr.* Rouget de Roche; *Ge.* Meerbarbe, Streifenbarbe; *It.* Triglia di Scoglio; *No.* Mulle; *Po.* Salmonete; *Sp.* Salmonete de Roca; *Sw.* Mullusen

This beautiful pink-and-gold fish of warmer waters has caused great confusion for scientists who now, mostly, agree that there are two species – this one inhabiting more northerly waters, the other, *Mullus barbatus*, found in more southerly waters. Both have two well-separated spiny dorsal fins, forked tail fins, pectoral fins directly under the pelvis, large, hard scales and two stiff barbels. *Surmuletus* alone has a distinct dark mark on the yellowish membrane of the first dorsal. It grows to 16 in. (40 cm). Of the goatfish, in warm waters the small red goatfish*, *Mullus auratus*, is most familiar in the western Atlantic.

Catch From its two barbel 'feelers', it is obvious that the red mullet is a bottom-feeder, living off crustaceans, shrimps, molluscs and worms; though never plentiful, they are taken on light tackle with appropriate bait. Bait should be presented on the bottom in the summer months on rocky shorelines (note the French and Spanish names) in the south and south west. Ancient legend has it that they were to be found in plenty after sea battles. De-scale soon after catching to preserve the red colour.

Cook Amongst the best of sea fish, red mullet are prized where they are to be found and are sometimes imported to Irish marble slabs and to Chinese supermarket freezers. Mullet are known to some as the woodcock of the sea, as they are traditionally, like the woodcock, grilled or baked without cleaning (though some snip off the gills). The red-haired Kelibians of Cap Bon in Tunisia – said to be descended from shipwrecked Irish – gut the unscaled fish through the gills, coat them with sea salt and grill.

Sea Bream

Red Sea Bream *Déargan Pagellus bogaraveo* Family: *Sparidae*

Am. Porgy*; *Da*. Spidstandet Blankesten; *Du*. Roode Zeebrasen; *Fr*. Rousseau, Dorade Commune; *Ge*. Nordischer Meerbrasen; *It*. Occhialone, Pagello; *Po*. Goraz; *Sp*. Besugo; *We*. Brôm y Môr

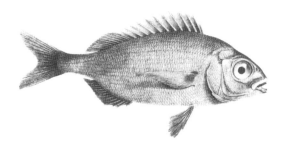

The red bream is not entirely red; indeed, sometimes it can be quite a greyish red. It reaches a length of about 20 in. (50 cm). The body is deep, the head profile steep. The single dorsal fin has anterior spines and it reveals a noticeable dark, diffused spot on the shoulder. To distinguish from other sea breams, examine the teeth. The red bream has sharp, curved teeth in the front of the jaws with two to three rows of rounded molars behind. Young fish may not have the shoulder patch. There are related porgies in the western Atlantic.

Black Bream *Bréan mara Spondyliosoma cantharus*

Da. Havrude; *Du*. Zeekarper; *Fr*. Brème de Mer, Dorade Grise; *Ge*. Seekarpfen; *It*. Tanuta; *No*. Havkarudse; *Po*. Choupa; *Sp*. Chopa

The black sea bream, or 'old wife', is dark grey with stripes and vertical bars. It has one row of sharp teeth.

Bogue *Boops boops*

Fr. Bogue; *Ge.* Gelbstriemen; *It.* Boga; *Po.* Boga; *Sp.* Boga

The bogue is silver with yellow longitudinal stripes and just one row of almost trefoil-shaped notched incisors. It grows up to 14 in. (35 cm).

Catch These three and occasional other sea visitors, such as the orange-red Pandora, *Pagellus erythrinus* – its back spotted with blue – the gilt head or daurade, *Sparus aurata* – with a golden-green bar across its forehead – and the Spanish bream, *Pagellus acarne* – which has a conspicuous black spot at the base of the pectoral – are not the commonest of Irish fish. However, global warming and their delicious sweet taste make them an attractive proposition for anglers who may catch those which escape French and Spanish boats. The Irish record for the red sea bream is 6 lb 6 oz (2.89 kg). A strip of squid on a long trace, fished over offshore shallows (4-6 fathoms – 9-10m) and reefs, will take black bream in southern waters. The more common red sea bream is taken in deeper waters, over reefs, around 15-20 fathoms (27-36 m).

Cook Grill small ones, slash the larger, marinate in lemon juice for 2 hours, then season. Bake in a buttered dish well sprinkled with basil, shallots, parsley, lemon slices and a generous splash of wine or beer.

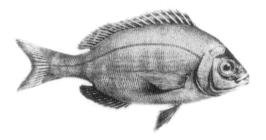

Black Sea Bream

Bogue

Pandora

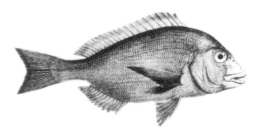

Gilt-Head / Daurade

Wrasse

Ballan Wrasse *Ballach breac* *Labrus bergylta* Family: *Labridae*

Am. Tautog*; *Da*. Berggylt; *Du*. Gevlekte Lipvis; *Fr*. Vielle, Labre; *Ge*. Gefleckter Lippfisch; *It*. Tordo Marvizzo; *No*. Berggylte; *Po*. Margota; *Sp*. Maragota, Duro; *Sw*. Berggylta; *We*. Gwrach

A heavy fish with heavy lips – hence some of its names – and heavy scales, the ballan wrasse has a single dorsal fin with spines in the anterior portion. The colour is a mottled green brown. The fin-ray formula is D XIX-XX/9-11, A III/8-10. A common fish, it grows to 10 lb (4.54 kg).

Cuckoo Wrasse *Ballach Muire* (*Muire* = Virgin Mary) *Labrus mixtus*

Da. Blåstak (male), Rødnaeb (female); *Fr*. Vielle Coquette, Labre Mêlé; *It*. Tordo Fischietto; *No*. As *Da*.; *Sp*. Gallano; *Sw*. Båstål

The fin-ray formula is D XVI-XVIII/11-14, A III/9-11, but most surely the distinguishing feature of this smaller wrasse is its bizarre colouring. The males are orange with bright blue heads and bright blue lines across the gill covers and along the sides. The females are red with three dark spots on the back, under and behind the dorsal fin. Their weight is 2 lb (0.9 kg).

Corkwing Wrasse *Bod gorm* (*bod* = penis, *gorm* = blue) *Crenilabrus melops*

Da. Savgylte; *Du*. Zwartoog-Lipvisch; *Fr*. Crénilabre; *Ge*. Schwarzäugiger Lippfisch; *It*. Tordo; *No*. Grönaade; *Sp*. Tordo; *Sw*. Skårsnultra

A much smaller wrasse, but still with the typical shape, the corkwing's fin-ray formula is D XV-XVIII/8-10, A III/8-10. The colours vary, usually a mottled greeny brown, but there can be streaks of blue or orange. There is an indistinct comma-like spot behind the eye and a much more distinct one at the base of the tail fin, below the lateral line. The corkwing grows to 8 oz (225 g).

Three other small wrasses are caught in Irish waters: the goldsinny, *Centrolabrus rupestris*, the rock or rock cook, *Centrolabrus exoletus*, and the rainbow, *Coris julius*. The rainbow's colours live up to its name; both of the others grow to around 6 in. (15 cm). The reddish goldsinny has one dark spot on the upper tail, another forward on the dorsal fin. The rock cook looks like a small corkwing. The fin-ray formula is D XVIII-XX/5-7, A IV-VI/6-8. Scales on the green-brown scale-rayed wrasse, *Acantholabrus palloni*, stray on to the fins. There is a blotch on the dorsal, another before the tail. Rare, it grows to 12 in. (30 cm).

Catch The corkwing is caught using mussel, limpet, crab and red eels off wave-smashed hard rocks. Be careful. Don't slip and don't get bitten by a big ballan.

Cook Excellent for soup, but fillets may be fried or poached in a court-bouillon and served with a strong gooseberry-based sauce.

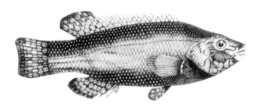

Ballan Wrasse

Cuckoo Wrasse (male)

Cuckoo Wrasse (female)

Wrasse

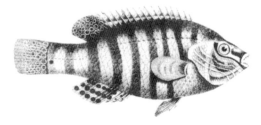

Corkwing Wrasse

Goldsinny

Rock Cook

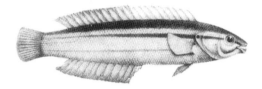

Rainbow Wrasse (female)

Rainbow Wrasse (male)

Scale-Rayed Wrasse

Sand-Eel

Greater Sand-Eel *Scadán gainimh, Corr gainimh* *Hyperoplus lanceolatus*
Family: *Ammodytidae*

Am. Sand Lance*; *Da*. Tobiskonge; *Du*. Groot Zandaal; *Fr*. Lançon; *Ge*. Grosser
Sandaal; *It*. Cicerello; *No*. Storsil; *Sp*. Pión

Growing up to 12 in. (30 cm), this is the largest of the five species of sand-eels
found in Irish waters. It is a slender, eel-like fish differing from the eels by having
long, low dorsal and anal fins and a small tail fin. The colour is green backed and
silvery bellied. It is always associated with sandy bottoms (the name in Irish
means 'sand herring') and up to 82 fathoms (150 m). It has a dark spot on the
side of its snout while the very similar *Hyperoplus immaculatus* has a uniformly
dark snout. It is rarely as abundant inshore as its smaller relation, the lesser
sand-eel – *Ammodytes tobianus* – or as common offshore as another lesser
sand-eel, *Ammodytes marinus*. The belly scales on the former form a chevron
pattern, those on the latter an irregular pattern. Scales are minute or absent from
the smooth sand-eel, *Ammodytes cicerellus*. The American and Pacific sand
lances*, *A. americanus* and *A. hexapterus*, are close relatives. The distantly
related 40 in. (100 cm) long black scabbard fish, *Aphanopus carbo*, excellent to
eat, will occur with increasing frequency on fishmongers' slabs.

Catch As staple food for herring, mackerel and the cod family, sand-eels are of
enormous importance in the food chain. They are also fished commercially. They
make excellent bait for sport-fishing. Sand-eels bury themselves in the sand and
can be caught scraping a vingler – a blunt-bladed hook-ended device – through
estuarial sands. A fine rake or a blunt hand sickle also works. Pigs root for them
at low tide. They are occasionally caught when sandy bottom-fishing with really
fresh bait.

Cook These tasty fish should be beheaded, dredged in flour and fried.

Weever

Lesser Weever *lasgán an ghaith nimhe* *Trachinus vipera* Family: *Trachinidae*

Da. Lille Fjaesing; *Du.* Kleine Pieterman; *Fr.* Petite Vive; *Ge.* Kleiner Petermann;
It. Tracina Vipera; *No.* Liten Fjesing; *Sp.* Salvariego

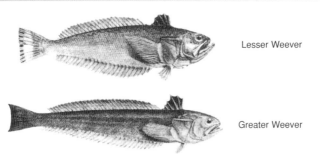

Lesser Weever

Greater Weever

Never greater than 6 in. (15 cm), the lesser weever has an unpleasant habit of burying itself in the sand in inshore waters. The bather knows nothing of this until an unshod pink foot encounters the sharp spines of the dorsal fins, which contain a quite unpleasantly powerful venom and which, apart from the top of the head, is the only part of the fish above sand. *Nimhe* means venomous in Irish. Ironically, its presence is a good indicator of clean beaches. Venom glands are also found on the gill covers, so handling this fish is something to be done carefully. A stout glove, which folds down the dorsal, is an essential. The wounds are extremely painful – first a sharp stab, then a pain which may increase in intensity for up to an hour and which may continue for up to twenty-four. The pain, at first localised, spreads to the entire limb. Death rarely ensues. Though distribution runs from the Mediterranean to Sweden, this species seems to be more prevalent in northern, rather than southern, Irish waters. The offshore greater weever, *Tracinus draco – Goineadoir mór* in Irish – pictured here is rare in the north. It has a black spot on the front dorsal fin; in the lesser weever the fin is entirely black.

Catch Should you really wish to, you should know that they feed at night.

Cook Cut off spines and head. Fillet; dip in batter and fry. Otherwise, braise in a buttered dish in a medium oven with an onion, tomato, lemon juice, white wine, seasoning, then top with cream for the last 5 minutes.

Mackerel

Mackerel *Ronnach   Scomber scombrus*
Family: *Scombridae*

Am. Atlantic Mackerel; *Da*. Makrel; *Du*. Makreel; *Fr*. Maquereau; *Ge*. Makrele; *It*. Sgombro, Maccarello; *No*. Makrell; *Po*. Sarda, Cavala; *Sp*. Caballa; *Sw*. Mackrill

This dazzling metallic-sheened torpedo of a fish is found in shoals from the Mediterranean to Iceland, and right up the western Atlantic seaboard. Its greeny-blue back is decorated with darker, waving strokes of colour; its belly is silvery white with absolutely no markings. It grows to 22 in. (55 cm). There appears to be confusion about the identity of a number of larger mackerel, referred to popularly as Spanish mackerel and/or chub mackerel. The Irish *Ronnagh Spáinneach* for the garfish (*see page 61*) confuses the situation again. Suffice it to say that the Spanish mackerel is larger, has a heavier head, a yellowing belly and, most importantly, oval spots on the lower sides. There are a number of other western Atlantic and Pacific species: the cero, chub, king, sierra and wahoo.

Catch As any fisherman knows, there is no problem catching mackerel once the fish are about, and they are most regularly caught on strings of feathers jigged off boats, or spun for, with silver bar-spoons, off rocks.

Cook The Romans thought mackerel good for jaundice, but these hearty-tasting fish are best cleaned and grilled, squirted with lemon juice – the only permissible diversion being to roll them in oatmeal first.

Spanish Mackerel

Spanish Mackerel

Tunny & Bonito

Tunny *Tuinnín* *Thunnus thynnus* Family: *Scombridae*

Am. Bluefin Tuna; *Da*. Tunfisk; *Du*. Tonijn; *Fr*. Thon Rouge; *Ge*. Thunfisch; *It*. Tonno; *No*. Makrellstørje; *Po*. Atum; *Sp*. Atún; *Sw*. Tonfisk

If you see a tunny in Irish waters, this is likely to be the one. They grow to over 12 ft (4 m), weigh up to 2,000 lb (900 kg) and are widely distributed across the oceans of the world. However, specimens in Irish waters are more likely to be less than 6 ft (2 m) long. The shape of all the tunnies and bonitos is distinctive: this one is coloured dark blue above with white sides, dotted with silver spots, and reveals a white belly. The dorsals are separated by only a tiny space.

Albacore *Tuinnín bán* *Thunnus alunga*

Ge. Germon; *Fr*. Thon Blanc; *It*. Tonno Bianco; *Sp*. Albacora

The albacore, or long-fin tunny, reaches a length of a metre and is easily distinguished by its long pectoral fins. Its colour is bronze with a lateral blue band. Some fins have spots. It can grow to 70 lb (32 kg).

Belted Bonito *Tuinnín stríocach Sarda sarda*

Am. Atlantic Bonito; *Da.* Rygstribet Pelamid; *Du.* Boniter; *Fr.* Pélamide; *Ge.* Pelamide; *It.* Palamita; *No.* Rygstribet Pelamide; *Po.* Bonito, Serrajão; *Sp.* Bonito

Even smaller, weighing only up to 12 lb (5.44 kg), the belted bonito's back is steel blue, swept obliquely with lots of dark-blue stripes. The sides and belly are silver.

Oceanic Bonito *Márín na smeach Katsuwonus pelamis*

Am. Skipjack Tuna; *Da.* Bugstripet Bonit; *Fr.* Bonite; *Ge.* Echter Bonito; *It.* Tonneto Striato; *No.* Bugstribet Bonit; *Sp.* Listado

With a stouter look about him and growing up to 40 lb (18 kg), the oceanic bonito's belly is distinctly marked with a series of parallel dark-blue stripes.

Plain Bonito *Auxis thazard*

Fr. Thazard; *It*. Tombarello; *Sp*. Melva

Sometimes called the frigate mackerel, the plain bonito has a corselet of pelvic scales.

Catch Fishing for tunny off the south west of Ireland is a developing sport among specialist skippers. Whole mackerel or herring, presented on a wire trace, are trolled or chummied.

Cook The flesh of all these fish is excellent (even in tins) but is best savoured when inch-thick (2.5 cm) fresh steaks are grilled, brushed with the minimum of butter or oil, scattered with rosemary, tarragon, salt and lots of freshly ground black pepper, and squirted with lemon juice just before serving. Or they can be fried, having been dredged in seasoned flour. Frozen steaks are quite acceptable, though they should be washed thoroughly in cold water when thawed to remove some of the blood. Really fresh flesh can be eaten raw, sliced very thinly. Tunny, or tuna, is excellent tossed in salads or to brighten an omelette.

Goby & Dragonet

Goby *Mac Siobháin* Family: *Gobiidae*

Da. Kutling; *Du.* Grondel; *Fr.* Gobie; *Ge.* Küling

Gobies found in Irish estuarial waters and intertidal rock pools include the 2.5 in. (6 cm) transparent goby, *Aphia minuta*, the 2.5 in. (6 cm) two-spotted goby, *Chaparrudo flavescens*, the 2 in. (5 cm) brilliantly spotted painted goby, *Gobius pictus*, the $2\frac{3}{4}$ in. (7 cm) common goby, *Gobius microps*, the 4 in. (10 cm) sandy-freckled sand goby, *Gobius minutus*, the 7 in. (17 cm) darkly mottled black goby, *Gobius niger*, and the 5 in. (12.5 cm) dark-brown rock goby, *Gobius paganellus*. They are often caught by patient, swift, childish hands. In Málaga and the Maritime Alps the transparent goby is considered a delight, dipped in beaten egg and fried.

Dragonet / Dusky Sculpin *lasgán nimhe*, *Scailpín Callionymus lyra*
Family: *Callionymidae*

Da. Stribet Fløjfisk; *Du.* Pitvisch; *Fr.* Lavandière; *Ge.* Leierfisch

Male

Female

The dragonet is one of three unmistakable species growing to 12 in. (30 cm), with startling fins and claw-like features on the cheeks. The fins are most notable in adult males, who also have bright ultramarine stripes and spots along their yellowish red-brown bodies, their cheeks and the lower part of their heads being orange with bright blue spots. Females and immature males are dullish brown and blotched on the back, paler beneath. The rarer spotted dragonet, *Callionymus maculatus*, has, in both sexes, spots on the dorsal fins. Caught, perchance, on muddy bottoms, the dragonet's flesh is white and firm. When cooking, fry.

Blenny

Blenny Family: *Blenniidae*

These families of tiny, stubby, slimy fish, their colours varying with the habitat, are widely distributed around Irish shores. The flesh is glutinous, but soup is possible.

Shanny *Ceann cruachain*, *Ceannruán Blennis pholis*

Da. Tangkvabbe; *Du*. Slijmfisch; *Fr*. Pholis; *No*. Tangkvabbe

The shanny has no head tentacles.

Butterfly Blenny *Blennius ocellaris*

Da. Øjeplettet; *Fr*. Blennie Papillon; *Ge*. Seeschmetterling

The butterfly blenny has a big spot on the dorsal fin.

Tompot *Blennius gattorugine*

Du. Slijmfisch; *Fr*. Perce-Pierre

The tompot has a branched tentacle over each eye.

Montagu's Blenny *Coyphoblennius galerita*

Fr. Blennie de Montagu

The Montagu's blenny has a curious eyebrow-like crest.

Butterfish *Sleamhnóg*, *Searróg Pholis gunnellus* Family: *Pholididae*

Da. Tangsprael; *Du*. Botervisch; *Fr*. Gronelle; *Ge*. Butterfisch

The 10 in. (25 cm) butterfish, brown, slim and slimy with a row of twelve spots, are under every rock.

Shanny

Tompot

Grey Mullet

Thick-Lipped Grey Mullet *Lannach* *Mugil chelo* Family: *Mugilidae*

Am. Striped Mullet*; *Da.* Multe; *Du.* Herder; *Fr.* Muge Noir, Mulet Lippu; *Ge.* Meeräsche; *It.* Bosega; *Sp.* Mujol Lisa

A powerful fish which makes tantalising swirls in estuarine waters, this grey mullet can reach a weight of 10 lb (4.54 kg), but those taken on the rod rarely go over half that weight. The upper lip looks thick and swollen, its greatest depth more than half the diameter of the eye. The local existence of the thin-lipped grey mullet, *Liza ramada*, is a matter of debate, as is that of the golden mullet, *Liza auratus*. The striped grey mullet, *Mugil cephalus*, appears both sides of the Atlantic. The white mullet, *Mugil curema*, is found in the western Atlantic only. The 6 in. (15 cm) green, silver-striped atherine, or sand-smelt, *Atherina presbyter*, is distantly related.

Catch Mullet will jump over the top of nets to the height of your shoulder when you are standing in the incoming tide. Nervous, or alert, creatures, they can be caught on rod and line with patience. Methods and baits vary from estuary to estuary, and local advice will be important. Mullet can be taken on the fly in one place, on bread pellets float-fished in another. Fishermen in Belfast Lough used to spread cow dung at low tide to attract them. I have seen a hole dug in the mud and filled with discarded cabbage to the same purpose. A rod-angler can lay a trail of bread pieces on the exposed silt leading to his position, where he waits for the tide with a 5 lb (2.3 kg) line and sliding float. There is a huge surge of energy when they hit.

Cook Fish taken far away from unpolluted harbours, piers and rivers are fine. Sauté or bake. Treat sand-smelts (also known as atherines) as whitebait.

Thick-Lipped Grey Mullet

Sand-Smelt

Gunard

Grey Gurnard *Cnúdán glas Eutrigla gurnardus* Family: *Triglidae*

Am. Sea-Robin*; *Da*. Grå Knurhane; *Du*. Grauwe Poon; *Fr*. Grondin Gris; *Ge*. Grauer Knurrhahn; *It*. Capone Gurno; *Po*. Ruivo; *No*. Knurr; *Sp*. Borracho; *Sw*. Knorrhane

Greyish red in colour, the body and head sprinkled with pale spots, the lateral line a prickly ridge, this astonishing-looking fish is quite common around Irish shores, reaching a top weight of 3 lb (1.36 kg). Its name in Spanish means 'drunkard' – maybe from its curious walk on the sea bottom. *Prionotus carolinus** and *Prionotus evolans** are confined to the western Atlantic.

Red Gurnard *Cnúdán dearg Aspitrigla gurnardus*

Da. Tvaerstribet Knurhane; *Du*. Engelsche Soldaat; *Fr*. Grondin Rouge; *It*. Capone Imperiale, Capone Coccio; *Sp*. Arete

The red gurnard's colour is deep red, the pelvic fins pink. As with all gurnards, the first few rays of the pectoral fins have developed into devices which act both as 'legs' and as tactile feelers. They reach 12 in. (30 cm). The larger deep-water piper, *Trigla lira – píobaire* in Irish – has a less-pronounced lateral line.

Tub Gurnard *Cnúdán gorm Trigla lucerna*

Da. Rød Knurhane; *Du*. Groote Poon; *Fr*. Galinette, Perlon; *Ge*. Roter Knurrhahn, Seeschwalbe; *It*. Capone Gallinella; *No*. Rødknurr; *Sp*. Bejel

The largest of the gurnards, reaching 24 in. (60 cm), the tub or saphirine is a dull red with a white belly and brilliant red pectoral fins, with blue-and-green spots.

Streaked Gurnard *Feochadán Trigloporus lastoviza*

Da. Bandet Knurhane; *Du*. Gestreepte Poon; *Fr*. Rouget Camard, Grondin Imbriago; *It*. Capone Ubriaco; *Sp*. Rubio

A rarish, reddish gurnard, with blue-and-yellow striped pectorals and striped feelers, the streaked gurnard grows to 14 in. (35 cm). The long-nosed armed gurnard is even rarer.

Catch Gurnard take worm, crab and shellfish bait from the sea bed.

Cook Be careful with spines. Fry fillets, or grill fish, wrapped in bacon.

Gunard

Grey Gunard

Red Gunard

Tub Gunard

Streaked Gunard

Armed Gunard

Sea Scorpion

Short-Spined Sea Scorpion   *Gréasaid cladaigh*   *Myoxocephalus scorpius*
Family: *Cottidae*

Am. Sculpin; *Da*. Almindelig Ulk; *Du*. Zeedonderpad, Botskop; *Fr*. Scorpion de Mer; *Fr. Canadian* Chaboisseau; *Ge*. Gemeiner Seescorpion; *It*. Scazzone; *No*. Marulk, Pelekunter; *We*. Sarph y Môr

Mottled brown and grey and green, bullheads are a family with broad, flat heads. They are found on both sides of the Atlantic, though not related to the American bullhead catfishes, *Ictaluridae*, and only distantly to members of the scorpion fish family, *Scorpaenidae*. Their small scaleless bodies are often covered with prickles. Ireland does not have the freshwater Miller's thumb, *Cottus gobbio*, but the 12 in. (30 cm) grey-mottled bull rout, short-spined sea scorpion or father lasher – with its striped fins – is common around Irish coasts.

Long-Spined Sea Scorpion   *Cottus bubalis*

Da. Langtornet Ulk; *Du*. Groene Zeedonderpad; *Fr*. Chabot de Mer; *Ge*. Seebull; *No*. Dvaergulk

This fish has longer spines, the uppermost of the pre-opercular spines being longer than the eye diameter. The lateral line is spiny. It grows to just 7 in. (17 cm).

Four-Horned Sea Scorpion   *Myoxocephalus quadricornis*

Sw. Hornsimpa

This one has four rough tubercules on the head, is grey brown on the back, yellow on the sides and dull white beneath. It is found on both sides of the Atlantic.

Norway Bullhead   *Taurlus lilljeborgi*

Da. Dvaergulk; *No*. Pigulk

This bullhead grows to 2.5 in. (6 cm), has greyish transverse bands on its yellowish body and is found in deeper waters.

Pogge / Armed Bullhead *Muiricín Agonus cataphractus* Family: *Agonidae*

Da. Panserulk; *Du.* Harnasmannetje; *Fr.* Souris de Mer; *Ge.* Steinpicker; *No.* Skjaegulk; *We.* Penbwl

Covered in bony plates, this 6 in. (15 cm) fish has many barbels under the chin.

Catch Not hunted specifically, these fish will take many small baits natural to their normal rocky-shored habitat, and in Greenland they are fished for with red beads. Beware venomous spines.

Cook Older books, such as Day's, write of the use of the flesh of the female *M. scorpius* (males were thought poisonous) in Greenland and of the use of *C. bubalis* in fish soups in Newfoundland. The Finns are really enthusiastic about fillets of *M. quadricornis (Härkäsimppu)* cooked as cod.

Short-Spinned
Sea Scorpion

Four-Horned
Sea Scorpion

Long-Spinned
Sea Scorpion

Pogge / Armed Bullhead

Lumpsucker

Lumpsucker *Léasán leice* *Cyclopterus lumpus* Family: *Cyclopteridae*

Da. Stenbider; *Du.* Snotdolf; *Fr.* Gros Mollet; *Ge.* Seehase; *It.* Cicloterro; *No.* Rognkjaeks; *Sw.* Stenbit (male), Kvabbso (female)

Also known variously as sea hen, hen-fish and, ingloriously, lump, the sole representative of this curious family of fish to be found in Irish waters is a bottom-feeding fish, whose feeding range runs from the extreme low tide mark to down to 160 fathoms (300 m). The young fish are frequently found in association with clumps of floating seaweed, which presumably aid in their dispersal. They come inshore in March to breed, the females returning to deep water afterwards, the males staying to guard the fertilised eggs. At up to 20 lb (9 kg) and 24 in. (60 cm) for females, and 20 in. (50 cm) for males, this normally grey, lumpy, bony fish with a sucker on the breast is, when caught accidentally on either side of the Atlantic, unmistakable. The head and the body are covered in bony bumps or denticles, and there are four rows of larger bony plates running longitudinally. When spawning, the male is blue above, brilliant orange below, just in case the female is not sure. The females are blue to very dark blue, the young emerald green or yellow. The sucker is used to attach to the sea bottom. It is taken occasionally off the north-east coast. The drab, diminutive sucker-fish, Montagu's sea snail, *Liparis Montagu*, of the family *Liparidae*, grows to 2.5 in. (6 cm). The 3 in. (8 cm) Connemara lumpsucker, *Lepadogaster – Candollei sumaire* in Irish – is no relation.

Catch Taken infrequently in trawls, the lumpsucker is capable of taking bait.

Cook Though eaten by sharks and rays, opinions vary on the quality of the flesh, some finding it disgustingly glutinous. Advice is that only the male's flesh is palatable, smoked in all seasons; the flesh of the female is said to be revolting in the breeding season – 'glue pudding' is the term to describe it. Sir Walter Scott infers it was prized in Edinburgh. The roe makes good 'caviar'.

Stickleback

Stickleback *Garmachán* *Gasterosteus aculeatus* Family: *Gasterosteidae*

Da. Trepigget Hundestejle; *Da.* Stekelbaars; *Fr.* Épinoche; *Ge.* Dreistachliger Stichling; *No.* Strikling

The most familiar and widespread of all European fish, the three-spined stickleback is found in all fresh waters (except rushing mountain streams) and in many estuaries, along the shore and out to sea. Colours vary from black to silver dorsally, white ventrally. The first two dorsal spines are prominent, the third tiny. It grows to 4 in. (10 cm), though most specimens are half that.

Ten- or Nine-Spined Stickleback *Garmachán dreich golipe* *Gasterosteus pugnitis*

Da. Nipigget Hundestejle; *Du.* Lille Hundestejle; *Fr.* Épinochette; *Ge.* Zwergstichling; *No.* Smaastickling

Usually 2 3/4 in. (7 cm) in length, this fish is confined to eastern Ireland and is less tolerant of salinity.

Fifteen-Spined Stickleback *Garmachán mara* *Spinachia spinachia*

Da. Tangsnarre; *Du.* Zee-Paddesteker; *Fr.* Épinoche de Mer; *Ge.* Seestickling; *No.* Tangstickling

Sometimes called the sea stickleback, this solitary creature is widespread, though by its nature (the other species are often found in huge shoals) is less often seen. Its habits are wholly marine, although it will tolerate estuarial waters. Its colouring seems to suit all its chosen habitats. It grows to 6 in. (15 cm). The stickleback's nest, woven in early summer amongst the branches of algae in a rock pool and composed of secretions and vegetable matter, can be as big as a man's hand.

Catch Catch in jam jars, little nets and with worms tied on strings.

Cook When waters were purer the shoals of the freshwater species were bigger, and they were netted as fodder for pigs, or winter feed for dogs. A nourishing soup is possible.

Flatfish

Turbot *Turbard Scolphthalmus maximus* Family: *Bothidae*

Am. Greenland Turbot*; *Da.* Pighvarre; *Du.* Tarbot; *Fr.* Turbot; *Ge.* Steinbutt; *It.* Rombo Chiodato; *No.* Piggvar; *Po.* Rodovalho, Pregado; *Sp.* Rodaballo; *Sw.* Piggvar

Flatfish are quite remarkable amongst vertebrates, departing from the usually pattern of having a body symmetrically arranged around the backbone. The first thing you notice is that they have both eyes close together on one side of the body and that only this particular side is coloured. The other is white. Flatfish are totally benthic; that is, they spend the whole of their life, once one eye has migrated at larval stage, on the sea bottom. Few, apart from the halibut, rise far in search of food. Curiously, sometimes the 'wrong' eye migrates, and the fish now has both eyes on what would be the blind side – but the colouration follows the dictate of the eye, and so the entire fish is the wrong way round. Typically, three families can be distinguished: *Bothidae* – eyes on the left; *Pleuronectidae* – eyes on the right; *Solidae* – eyes on the right, mouth to one side of the head. The Irish record for the big diamond-shaped sandy-coloured turbot is 34 lb (15.4 kg), caught in Cork harbour; but the best specimens are taken, generally, off the Causeway Coast. The turbot has no scales, but a series of bony tubercules across its back. Neither the diamond turbot from the Pacific nor the Greenland turbot* is a true turbot.

Catch Fished over sandy or gravelly bottoms, from the sea shore out to 44 fathoms (80 m), turbot feed on sprats, sand-eels, pouting, haddock and poor cod, and not, as many anglers think, invertebrates. The best baits are sand-eels or long thin strips of fresh white mackerel belly.

Cook Farmed fish are of interest. The rich, the obsessive or lucky inheritors have a *turbotière* in which to poach this really delicious fish whole. Serve with a simple hollandaise sauce. Grill small ones whole.

Brill *Broit Scophthalmus rhombus* Family: *Bothidae*

Am. Windowpane*; *Da.* Slethvarre; *Du.* Greit, Kaan; *Fr.* Barbue; *Ge.* Kleist, Glattbutt; *It.* Rombo Liscio; *No.* Slettuar; *Po.* Rodovalho, Patrúcia; *Sp.* Rémol; *Sw.* Slätvar

Brill is a rugby-ball shaped fish the colour of wet sand, which brings back memories of summers spent paddling the strand. It can grow to a length of 2 ft (60 cm), but most you will see will be half that. The sandy side is spotted with dark freckles and lighter spots. Scientists will tell you that the brill's eyes are on the left of its face, though the plain people of Ireland can see, plainly enough, that its mouth, with its tiny teeth, is to the left of its eyes. The lateral line has a strong curve just behind the head. If the fishmonger offers you a turbot with no bumps on its brown back, he's passing you off with a broit. So run your fingers down his spine – the broit's, that is, not the fishmonger's.

Catch The brill is found in the Mediterranean and in coastal waters from Portugal to Norway. The related American windowpane, *Scophthalmus aquosus*, has less flesh. Trawlers land a few hundred tonnes of brill in Irish ports each year, leaving some for sport-anglers who catch them, mostly in summer, drifting over shallow, sandy banks. Anglers use a flowing trace, with lots of red-and-yellow attractor beads, above a silver spoon with a long-shanked number 2 hook, baited with ragworm and held on by a sliver of white mackerel belly or squid. They are targeting plaice, but catch the occasional brill. The Irish record stands at 9.8 lb (4.313 kg), and Belmullet, the Causeway Coast and Crookhaven are good bases.

Cook Fish caught during the spring spawning season can be lacking in flavour. Wash, pat dry with kitchen paper, grill smaller ones whole on the bone, after cleaning, with a little fat from fried bacon. Keep the resulting crisped bacon to crack and scatter over the fish, served white-side up with lemon juice, a sprig of parsley and new boiled potatoes.

Megrim / Sail-Fluke/Whiff *Sciolteán Lepidorhombus whiffiagonis*
Family: *Bothidae*

Da. Glashvarre; *Du*. Sharretong; *Fr*. Caradine; *It*. Giallo; *Po*. Areeiro, Pregado; *Sp*. Lliseria; *No*. Glasflyndre; *Sw*. Glasvar

Less rhomboid than the turbot and narrower, with a straighter mouth, its lower eye in advance of its upper one, the pinkish-brown megrim is a deep-water fish attaining 24 in. (60 cm). It eats flatfish, sand-eels, dragonets, shrimp, crab and squid. The megrim and its half-size look-alike relative *Lepidorhombus boscii*, with two spots each on dorsal and anal fins, are targets for trawlers.

Topknot *Leathóg lice Zeugopterus punctatus*

Da. Hårkvarre; *Fr*. Targeur, Sole des Rochers; *It*. Cornetto; *No*. Bergvar; *Sp*. Caracol Gris

With its beautiful mottling, this topknot appears to have bushy eyebrows. It grows to 10 in. (25 cm).

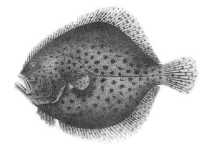

Turbot

Brill

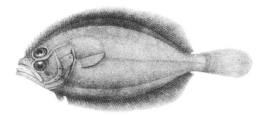

Megrim / Sail-Fluke / Whiff

Ekstrom's Topknot/Bloch's Topknot *Phrynorhombus regius*

Whether the honours go to Bloch or Ekstrom, this small – 8 in. (20 cm) – diffusely mottled fish has a distinct notch on its snout. The Norwegian topknot, *Phrynorhombus norvegicus*, 5 in. (12 cm), has a smooth snout and irregular blotches.

Scaldfish *Leathóg scalladh Arnoglossus laterna*

Da. Tungehvarre; *Du*. Schurftvis; *Fr*. Sole Maudite, Fausse Limande; *Ge*. Lammzunge; *It*. Suacia; *No*. Tungevar; *Sp*. Serrandell

This small 7 in. (18 cm) fish, and several close relatives, has mottled skin and scales which rub off easily.

Catch / Cook Caught accidentally, these fish are worth cooking as you would with plaice.

Dab *Leatha riabhac, Daba Limanda limanda* Family: *Pleuronectidae*

Am. Rusty Dab*; *Da*. Slette; *Du*. Schar; *Fr*. Limande; *Ge*. Kleische; *It*. Limanda; *No*. Sandflyndre; *Sp*. Limanda; *Sw*. Sandskädda

This family of fish have their eyes on the right side of the body – the mouth is to the right of the eyes when you hold the fish, head pointing away from you. They range in habitat from shoreline and up estuaries, to deep water, and eight different species are recorded for Irish waters. Popular names for the fish vary, and there is a great overlap, due as much to the avarice of fishmongers and restaurateurs (passing off a fish as a cousin of its betters), as to lack of knowledge. There is as much confusion in North America as in Europe. The true dab, with its overall sandy colouring, freckled with brown and yellow, can be detected easily by the pronounced curve in the lateral line just behind the head and over the pectoral fin. They can grow to over 2 lb (0.9 kg) and 10 in. (25 cm) long.

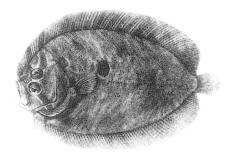

Topknot

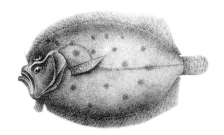

Ekstrom's Topknot / Bloch's Topknot

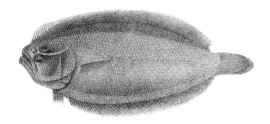

Scaldfish

Flatfish

Flounder *Dubh-leatha Platichthys flesus*

Da. Skrubbe; *Du*. Bot; *Fr*. Flet; *Ge*. Flunder; *It*. Passera Pianuzza; *No*. Skrubbe;
Po. Patruça; *Sp*. Platija; *Sw*. Skrubba; *We*. Lleden Fach

The flounder, or fluke, grows to 22 in. (55 cm). The lateral line is hardly curved;
the colour is green to brown with dull-orange flecks. There are American
relations.

Lemon Sole *Leathóg buí, Leathóg mhin Microstomus kitt*

Da. Rødtunge; *Du*. Tongschar, Steenschol; *Fr*. Sole Limande; *Ge*. Rotzunge;
No. Lombre; *Sp*. Mendo Limón; *Sw*. Bergtunga

A dull-looking fish, brownish with irregular markings and mottlings in dark brown,
orange and green (it is not even a true sole), the lemon sole has a tiny head and
a slimy feel. It grows to 26 in. (65 cm) and lies on sand banks at 20 to 110
fathoms (40–200 m), mostly north west of Ireland. It tastes good and is of
commercial importance, but will not take bait.

Witch/Pole Dab *Leathóg bhán Glyptocephalus cynoglossus*

Am. Witch Flounder, Gray Sole; *Da*. Skærising; *Du*. Hondstrong; *Fr*. Plie Grise;
Ge. Zungenbutt; *No*. Smørflyndre; *Sw*. Mareflundra

The pole dab is grey brown, with the tiniest of black spots and a straight lateral
line.

Rough Dab *Leathóg garbh, Daba gorm Hippoglossoides platessoides
limandoides*

Am. American Plaice*; *Da*. Håising; *Du*. Lange Schar; *Fr*. Fausse Sole, Sole
d'Écosse; *Ge*. Scharbenzunge; *No*. Gapeflyndre; *Sw*. Lerskadda

As the name indicates, this grey-red fish has obvious large, rough-edged scales.

Catch / Cook *See pages 89 and 92 – as for Wrasse or Greater Sand-Eel.*

Dab

Flounder

Lemon Sole

Plaice *Leathóg bhreac, Leathóg bhallach* Family: *Pleuronectidae*

Am. American Plaice*; *Da*. Rødspette; *Du*. Schol; *Fr*. Plie, Carrelet; *Ge*. Scholle; *It*. Passera; *No*. Rødspette; *Po*. Solha; *Sp*. Solla, Platija; *Sw*. Rödspotta; *We*. Lleden

A most beautiful fish, dark sandy brown with wonderful red-orange spots and a row of palpable knobs behind the head, the delicious plaice grows to 36 in. (90 cm), but is usually caught, unfortunately, and sold at around half that size. It is found from shallow water to depths of around 66 fathoms (120 m), mostly on sandy, but occasionally over muddy, ground. Sometimes plaice will venture into estuaries. The range is from Norway to Cadiz, and they may also be found in the Mediterranean. Plaice can live up to twenty years, by which time they are often 24 in. (60 cm). At nine years of age they measure 16 in. (40 cm), then putting on $\frac{3}{4}$ in. (1.5 cm) a year. Related American plaice*, *Hippoglossoides platessoides*, have less flesh.

Catch Larger plaice eat mussels, dog whelks, razor-fish, shore crab, hermit crab and both rag- and lugworm, and feed mainly during the daylight hours – which is a happy circumstance for most anglers. It is commercially the most important flatfish around Irish coasts, but luckily there are still good catches for charter-boats off the south and north coasts, though shore-caught plaice are scarce. Ballycotton and Portrush are good bases. Boats are drifted over offshore banks, trailing and bouncing attractor beads and spoons on a long trace along the sand, intriguing the plaice. Baits are usually a bunch of rag or lug on a long-shanked hook, held on with the tiniest tippet of white mackerel belly. Let the fish take a good munch before you strike.

Cook The recipe for small brill (*see page 111*) is excellent for plaice. Otherwise skin them, prepare a mixture of 3 oz (85 g) butter, the juice of a small lemon, sea salt, fresh-ground black pepper and 2 tbsp chopped tarragon. Rub this on the skinned fish, then grill. Bigger fish can be simmered in a court-bouillon and served with a gooseberry or raspberry sauce. Or you could nip down to the chip shop.

Witch / Pole Dab

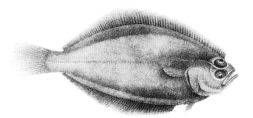

Rough Dab

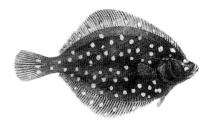

Plaice

Halibut *Bó-leatha*, *Haileabó* *Hippoglossus hippoglossus*
Family: *Pleuronectidae*

Am. Atlantic Halibut; *Da*. Helleflynder; *Du*. Heilbot; *Fr*. Flétan; *Ge*. Heilbutt; *It*. Halibut; *No*. Kveite; *Sp*. Halibut; *Sw*. Hälleflundra

This rare deep-water monster from both sides of the Atlantic is usually identified by its huge size, growing to 100 in. (2.54 m) with a weight of 700 lb (315 kg). The blind side is pearly white, the upper side a dark green. Halibut can reach thirty-five years of age, and the large mature males are taken off the edge of the continental shelf. Females and immature fish are found in 60 fathoms (110 m) of water over sandy, gravelly or rocky ocean banks. Unlike other flatfish, the halibut will forage upwards in search of food, which consists of herring, haddock and cod. On the bottom they feed on flatfish, spider crab and lobster. No wonder the flesh tastes so good. The much rarer 40 in. (100 cm), 20 lb (9 kg) Greenland halibut, *Reinharditus hippoglossoides*, which is not a true halibut, has a browner colour, and the blind side is also heavily pigmented.

Catch Considering its size, Day's observation that halibut was normally taken on strong hooks and lines seems superfluous. His record that the baits used were whelks and wrasse and that the season was winter is more useful. Rocky areas with strong tide-races are recommended. The Irish record fish of 156 lb (70.2 kg) was taken off Belmullet, and other big ones have been taken off Valentia. Tackle will include Clements boom, terminal wire trace, big silver attractor spoons and big, fresh bait. Commercial longliners say the fish does not fight hard – until boated.

Cook The flesh is inclined to be dry, though of good flavour. The white (when cooked) flesh has a large-flaked, dense texture, a low fat content and can be cooked in any manner. Bake steaks in foil, thus poaching with no loss of flavour, with celery, carrot, onion, butter, dill and seasoning. A dash of poteen, were it legal, would perfect this dish.

Sole *Sól*, *Sól dubh*, *Leathóg dubh* *Solea solea* Family: *Soleidae*

Da. Tunge; *Du*. Tong; *Fr*. Sole; *Ge*. Zunge; *No*. Tunge; *Po*. Linguado; *Sp*. Lenguado; *Sw*. Tunga

Many fish are called sole, but only the European Dover, or black, is the most sought after of table fish. The Dover is sepia coloured with darker blotches, which disappear soon after death. The pectoral fin has an elliptical dark spot on

Halibut

Sole

Solenette

its upper edge, running right to the margin of the fin. It can reach a length of 20 in. (50 cm). It is the most common of the soles in these waters, coming inshore in warmer weather and wintering deep.

The lemon sole (*see page 116*) is not a true sole, and neither of the two Pacific soles, the Dover, *Microstomus pacificus*, and the English, *Parophrys vetulus*, are related to the European sole.

Solenette *Sól beag Solea lutea*

Da. Glastunge; *Du*. Dwergtong; *Fr*. Solenette; *Ge*. Zwergzunge

This tiny 3 in. (8 cm) fish is sandy yellow, and each fifth or sixth dorsal and anal fin ray is black.

Thickback Sole *Sól stríocha Microchirus variegatus*

Fr. Pole Panachée

Thickset and of a chestnut colour crossed by five darker bands, this inshore fish, which grows to 10 in. (25 cm), is a visitor from warmer waters.

Sand Sole *Sól ghainimh Pegusa lascaris*

Du. Fransetong, Zandtong; *Fr*. Sole Pôle; *It*. Sogliola dal Porro; *Po*. Linguada da Areia; *Sp*. Sortija

Sandy coloured with dark freckles and a dark spot on the pectoral fin not reaching the fin's edge, this warm-water sole grows to 14 in. (35 cm).

Catch Dover sole can be taken at night when feeding over sand and gravel on crustacea and small marine worms. Ballycotton has a good reputation. Flowing traces and tiny worm baits are usual.

Cook Toss chopped shallots and mushrooms in a buttered pan. Place your sole fillets on top and scatter more mushrooms, seasoning and chopped parsley over them. Add a big glass of dry wine or cider or beer and poach, cooking the fish and reducing the liquid. Meanwhile have your cooking companion blend 2 tbsp butter and 3 tbsp flour to add to the reduced liquid. Add a squirt of lemon. Serve the liquid over the fish: *sole bonne femme*.

Thickback Sole

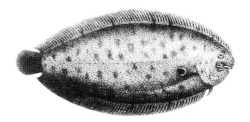

Sand Sole

Anglerfish

Anglerfish *Láimhíneach, Iascaire Lophuis piscatorus* Family: *Lophiidae*

Am. Goosefish*; *Da.* Bredflab; *Du.* Zeeduivel; *Fr.* Baudroie, Lotte; *Ge.* Seeteufel; *It.* Rospo, Rana Pescatrice; *No.* Havtask; *Po.* Peixe Sapo, Ra do Mar; *Sp.* Rape; *Sw.* Havspadda

Mottled reddish brown for camouflage, this vast fish hides half burrowed in the sandy bottom, dangling and manipulating the waving rays on its head to attract, as one would with a fishing-rod and lure, curious small fish to their doom. The skin is loose, the head vast, and the big posteriorly curved teeth are hinged so that they fold back to let a fish in, then snap back up to trap. Length can be up to 78 in. (195 cm). The Irish record fish of 94.6 lb (42.99 kg) was caught in Belfast Lough in 1985. The American goosefish, *Lophius americanus*, is very closely related. The first of the translated names in Irish refers to its hand-like fins, the second means 'fisherman'. The Dutch and Germans see the anglerfish as a 'sea devil', the Italians as a 'frog-fish', the Portuguese as both 'toad-fish' and 'frog-fish'; the Americans see it as stuffing itself like a goose. The common French name, *lotte*, is more appropriately used for the burbot, a rare freshwater cod not found in Ireland.

Catch Too rare inshore to spark targeted hunting, anglerfish are caught on large (whole fish) baits bottom-fished. Beware of the hinged teeth when attempting to remove the hook.

Cook A fish with splendid flesh, sold by unscrupulous restaurateurs as lobster, on occasion, its tail should be removed, skinned and the membrane pulled from the flesh, which is then split and grilled.

Alternatively, it can be stuffed and baked as for lamb. It is usually and quite erroneously sold in fishmongers and restaurants as the much rarer monkfish (*see page 28*). Because of its lack of bones and generally unfishy qualities, it is much favoured by those who do not like fish but who wish to join with fish eaters in fashionable circumstances.

Bibliography

Ainmneach Plandaí Agus Ainmhithe (An Gúm, 1978).

An Bord Iascaigh Mhara, *Annual Reports*, various.

Baker, J., *Simply Fish* (Faber & Faber, 1988).

Beard, J., *James Beard's New Fish Cookery* (Little Brown, 1976).

Davidson, A., *North Atlantic Seafood* (Macmillan, 1979).

Davidson, A., *Mediterranean Seafood* (Penguin, 1972).

Day, F., *The Fishes of Great Britain and Ireland* (Williams and Northgate, 1880-84).

Day, F., *British and Irish Salmonidae* (Williams and Northgate, 1887).

F.A.O. (Food and Agriculture Organisation of the United Nations), *Peces de Aquas Continentales de Europa* (Catálogo Multilingüe, 1971).

Farran, G.P., 'Local Irish Names of Fishes,' *Irish Naturalists' Journal*, Vol. VIII, Nos 9-12 (1946).

Ferguson, A., 'Systematics of Irish Charr (Electroporesis),' *Biochemical Systematics and Ecology*, Vol. 9 (Pergammon, 1981).

Ferguson, A. et al, 'Brown trout populations of Lough Melvin, Ireland [Genetic Differentiation]', *Biological Journal of the Linnean Society* (1991).

First Report of the Commissioners of Inquiry of the Irish Fisheries (Thom, 1884).

Grigson, J., *Fish Cookery* (Penguin, 1975).

Holt, E.W.L., *The Freshwater Eel* (Fisheries Ireland, Sci. Invest., 1907).

Houghton, W., *British Fresh-Water Fishes* (Hull and York, 1895).

Irish Specimen Fish Committee Report (1990).

Irish Sport Fishes: A Guide to their Identification (Iontaobhas Lascaigh Intire Ioncorportha), undated.

K'eogh, A.B., *Zoologiina Medicalis Hibernica* (Powell, 1739).

McClane, A.J., *McClane's Fish Buyer's Guide* (Henry Holt, 1990).

Phillips, R. and Rix, M., *Freshwater Fish of Britain, Ireland and Europe* (Pan, 1985).

Reports on the Sea and Inland Fisheries of Northern Ireland (HMSO), various.

Sharff, R.F., 'Irish Names of Reptiles, Amphibians and Fishes,' *Irish Naturalists' Journal* (July 1916).

Thompson, W., *The Natural History of Ireland* (London, 1856).

Walton, I., *The Compleat* [sic] *Angler* (1633, reprinted by Penguin, 1939).

Went, A.E.J. and Kennedy, M., *List of Irish Fishes* (S.O., 1976).

Wheeler, A., *The Fishes of the British Isles and North-West Europe* (Macmillan, 1969).

Wilson, J.P.F., *Postglacial Colonisation of Ireland by Fish*, *[etc]* (Irish Biogeographical Society).

Further Information:

An excellent source of information on Irish Record fish catches is the Irish Specimen Fish Committee.

Their web-site is www.irish-trophy-fish.com